Reading Poetry in the Middle Grades

▶ Reading Poetry in the Middle Grades

20 Poems and Activities That Meet the Common Core Standards and Cultivate a Passion for Poetry

Paul B. Janeczko

Heinemann
Portsmouth, NH

Heinemann
361 Hanover Street
Portsmouth, NH 03801–3912
www.heinemann.com

Offices and agents throughout the world

Library of Congress Cataloging-in-Publication Data
Janeczko, Paul B.
    Reading poetry in the middle grades : 20 poems and activities that meet the common core standards and cultivate a passion for poetry / Paul B. Janeczko.
        p. cm.
    ISBN-13: 978-0-325-02710-4
    ISBN-10: 0-325-02710-2
    1. Poetry—Study and teaching (Middle school)—United States. 2. Creative writing (Middle school)—United States. 3. Language arts—Correlation with content subjects. I. Title.

    LB1631.J366 2011
    808.1071'2—dc22   2010041007

Editors: Wendy M. Murray and Lisa Luedeke
Production: Victoria Merecki
Cover and interior designs: Lisa A. Fowler
Typesetter: Kim Arney
Manufacturing: Valerie Cooper

Printed in the United States of America on acid-free paper

17   16   15   PAH   5   6

for Bob Skapura
over the years, across the miles
my Mac guru, my WebGuy, my friend

▶ CONTENTS

Paul Janeczko has been a poetry ambassador for many years. His anthologies have helped teachers navigate the many new and sometimes unknown voices in contemporary poetry. If you love poetry, you've probably read at least one of Paul's brilliant anthologies as well as his own excellent poetry.

I first found one of Paul's anthologies over twenty years ago; I thought it was one of the best anthologies of contemporary poetry for young adults I had ever read. As he published more anthologies over the years, I knew Paul had a gift. He has a remarkable, unerring ear for really good poems. You can imagine the thrill I felt when Paul asked me to write a foreword for this book.

Over the years, Paul and I have become friends. His voice in this book is very much like his voice in person: friendly, to the point, always propelled by a keen sense of humor. It's that voice that guides us through the twenty poems he's selected. Listen to him describe how a poem should work in this short sentence: *All the parts should make the poem purr, snarl, crackle, laugh, rumble, or roar.*

We trust Paul, not just because of his track record, but because we know from the way he writes that he is a teacher. Paul taught high school English for many years and is expert at knowing how to invite both teachers and students into the sometimes foreign world of poetry.

Paul has chosen the poems in *Reading Poetry in the Middle Grades: 20 Poems and Activities That Meet the Common Core Standards and Cultivate a Passion for Poetry* with his usual care. The range is brilliant, from contemporary poets like Ted Kooser, the former Poet Laureate of the United States, to classic poets like Robert Frost and William Blake.

He then uses a repeating blueprint to help us traverse the landscape of each poem. We learn about a poem's reason for being, we're told about it's structure and poetic elements, we're shown how to listen to the music of the poem, and, in one of my favorite sections, After Reading: Knowing the Poem Forever, we explore the poem's "truths and ideas" that are "portals to a deeper exploration."

One of the ways Paul invites students to become active learners is through graphic organizers that help students know a poem from the inside out. For example, he asks students to draw a scene from Mark Vinz's mysterious "Deserted Farm" to deepen their understanding of the poem. Imagery is a perfect doorway into their appreciation.

By the time you finish reading and teaching from *Reading Poetry in the Middle Grades: 20 Poems and Activities That Meet the Common Core Standards and Cultivate a Passion for Poetry*, you and your students will feel as if you have traveled to twenty new countries with Paul, met new friends and old, and become infinitely wiser about the world of poetry.

Georgia Heard

▶ ACKNOWLEDGMENTS

Thank you to my merry band of Lit Divas: Susan Bean, Connie Burns, Cindy Christin, Donna Knott, and Carole Koneff.

Thank you to Judy Wallis for offering her professional perspective and suggestions to the project.

▶ INTRODUCTION

First, an admission: I wish the culture today was one in which I didn't have to work so hard to convince others that poetry counts. On a lot of levels. When a poem is presented well, you'll see students who have been quiet suddenly look up, speak up. The poem has awakened something. A few days later, you might discover alliteration showing up in students' writing, or unusual word choice, or sentence variety. In the midst of a literature discussion, a student might refer to a poem you just read, taken by surprise that poet and novelist painted the mood in the same way, or had arrestingly different takes on prejudice, love, or loss.

As teachers today, everything we teach has to be turbocharged with skills and the promise of advancing our students academically. I know that. And here's the cool thing: poetry can get you there. It is inherently turbocharged. Poets distill a novel's worth of content and emotion in a handful of lines. The literary elements and devices you need to teach are all there, powerful and miniature as a bonsai tree. So in this book, I have gathered twenty poems that students tend to love and, for each one, lesson ideas that help you meet language arts requirements. The signature feature that sets this book apart from others is a response sheet in the form of a graphic organizer. In my work in classrooms, I've found there is something about the openness of these organizers that helps students jump over their fear of a poem and dive into personal, smart, analytical responses.

I am confident that by book's end you'll see lots of ways to bring poetry more often to your teaching, but for now, I want to touch upon two "high demand" challenges the lessons in this book were written to address:

- Student Engagement
- The Common Core Standards for English Language Arts

Student Engagement

If our students aren't motivated to learn, we can take our marbles and go home. Nothing we read aloud or model will stick if they are disengaged by the content or stay silent because our talk is overtaking too much of our day together. For years, we've talked about the crisis of student engagement, and yet we seem to spin our wheels when it comes to changing our teaching to provide the experiences and interactivity that lead to engagement. Personally, my own change as a teacher often comes about after I've talked to one inspiring colleague, tried one new activity with students, or read one book that really engaged me. In other words, none of us needs to swim a sea of professional resources; just find a couple you trust and go forward—now. For inspiration, Daniel Pink's new book, *Drive*, reminds us that creating a state of flow is critical to learning and engagement. If you're not familiar with the research on flow, the groundbreaking book, *Flow: The Psychology of Optimal Experience* by Mihaly Csikszentmihalyi, is another must-read. For considering lesson design, I recommend reading the work of Judith Langer. A researcher who has done a great deal of work in grades 6–12, Langer suggests four principles for creating an engaging classroom. As you read the lessons in this book, you will see how they mirror these four principles:

1. **Social interactions** are focused on students thinking about what they know, the ideas they are developing, where they situate themselves as learners. Students are treated as a capable, lifelong learners.

2. **Questions are central** to experiences. They invite students to reflect, explore, and move ahead.

3. **The students look ahead (not back at what they once thought) toward the new ideas** they can develop. Every action—reading, writing, thinking (alone or with a group)—pushes students toward new learning.

4. **Multiple perspectives are considered**—growing naturally out of differing goals, values, experiences, and understandings.

The Common Core Standards for English Language Arts

The poems and activities possess the themes, swift pacing, ownership, and chance for collaboration that preteens and adolescents need in order to learn best. Try them with your students—I think you'll discover a high level of engagement. But the second critical need we have as teachers is to assure that we are using literature content to enhance students' reading, writing, and thinking as outlined by state, local, and national standards. To help you see how the poems and activities in this book address the common core standards for English language arts, I created the chart in Figure 1. It's by no means complete—there are more poems and lessons in this book that hit these and other standards too. But I share it to get you thinking about how you can quite easily look up the standards online and create your own grid of matching content and teaching to them. Listening and Speaking is another category of the ELA standard that is beautifully answered by poetry and its oral tradition; in fact the Say It Out Loud section for each poem in this book abounds with creative ways to develop students' ability to "think on their feet" and perform.

English Language Arts Standards for Reading: Literature	Lessons and Activities

KEY IDEAS AND DETAILS

1. QUOTE ACCURATELY from a text when explaining what the text says explicitly and when drawing inferences from the text.

"A Poison Tree"
- **Tone organizer:** reading poem and answering questions about the feelings of narrator.

"Speak Up"
- **Noticing Character:** reading poem and making inferences about both speakers.

2. DETERMINE A THEME OF A STORY, drama, or poem from details in the text, including how characters in a story or drama respond to challenges or how the speaker in a poem reflects upon a topic; summarize the text.

"Friends in the Klan"
- **Getting to Know the Poem:** students respond to the theme of courage in terms of how Carver responded to threats by the Klan.

"Junkyards"
- **Meeting the Poem:** students discuss the notion of "progress" and the poet's attitude toward it.

3. COMPARE AND CONTRAST two or more characters, settings, or events in a story or drama, drawing on specific details in the text (e.g., how characters interact).

"When It Is Snowing"
"Poppies"
- **Details and Senses organizer:** students compare and contrast the sense details used in each poem.

"Every Cat Has a Story"
- **Sense Details organizer:** students compare and contrast the attributes of the cats described in the poem.

CRAFT AND STRUCTURE

4. DETERMINE THE MEANING OF WORDS and phrases as they are used in a text, including figurative language such as metaphors and similes.

"Tugboat at Daybreak"
- **Noticing Figurative Language:** students explore the metaphors that Morrison uses.

"Spring Storm"
- **Noticing Figurative Language:** students explore the central metaphor of a storm.

5. EXPLAIN HOW a series of chapters, scenes, or stanzas fits together to provide the overall structure of a particular story, drama, or poem.

"A Poison Tree"
- **Noticing Plot organizer:** students fill in plot boxes to identify the parts of the narrative of the poem.

"The Wreck of the *Hesperus*"
- **Noticing Plot organizer:** students fill in episode blocks to outline the narrative arc of the ballad.

6. DESCRIBE how a narrator's or speaker's point of view influences how events are described.

"Ode to Family Photographs"
- **Noticing Mood:** students examine the family photos as a window into family life.

4

CRAFT AND STRUCTURE *(continued)*

"Hoods"
- **Noticing Figurative Language:** Students explore how the figurative language of the narrator conveys his point of view.

INTEGRATION OF KNOWLEDGE AND IDEAS

7. **ANALYZE HOW** visual and multimedia elements contribute to the meaning, tone, or beauty of a text (e.g., graphic novel, multimedia presentation of fiction, folktale, myth, poem).

"Tugboat at Daybreak"
- **Noticing Mood:** students discuss how the sense details create a sense of quiet.

"Foul Shot"
- **Noticing Active Verbs:** students examine the sequence of action in the poem.

8. **COMPARE AND CONTRAST** stories in the same genre (e.g., mysteries and adventure stories) on their approaches to similar themes and topics.

"Abandoned Farmhouse"
"Deserted Farm"
- Students examine the similarities between the setting in these poems.

RANGE OF READING AND COMPLEXITY OF TEXT

9. **BY THE END OF THE YEAR,** read and comprehend literature, including stories, dramas, and poetry, at the high end of the grades 4–5 text complexity band independently and proficiently.

Figure 1

Poems: Perfect Short Texts for Teaching Literary Elements

The grid in Figure 2 gives an aerial view, if you will, of the poems in this book and the craft techniques and literary elements they provide models of. I love how the format invites me to "plug in" new connections that might occur. For example, think about how a particular poem works beautifully with a particular passage in a novel or piece of nonfiction to show students imagery, metaphor, or foreshadowing. Use this grid as a starting point to help you layer your teaching across genres.

The Lifetime Benefits of Learning to Read Poetry

Beyond engagement and standards, I want this book to work in a timeless way to help you and your students read poetry with ease. Sure, it counts for teaching reading and writing skills, but above all, poetry counts in nourishing ourselves and our

Figure 2

ELEMENT \ POEM	"Abandoned Farmhouse," by Ted Kooser	"Deserted Farm," by Mark Vinz	"When It Is Snowing," by Siv Cedering, and "Poppies," by Roy Scheele	"Speak Up," by Janet S. Wong	"A Poison Tree," by William Blake	"Summertime Sharing," by Nikki Grimes	"The Wreck of the Hesperus," by Henry Wadsworth Longfellow	"Every Cat Has a Story," by Naomi Shihab Nye	"Street Painter," by Ann Turner	"Seeing the World," by Steven Herrick	Four Haiku, by J. Patrick Lewis	"Tugboat at Daybreak," by Lillian Morrison	"Ode to Family Photographs," by Gary Soto	"Hoods," by Paul B. Janeczko	"Friends in the Klan," by Marilyn Nelson	"Spring Storm," by Jim Wayne Miller	"Foul Shot," by Edwin A. Hoey	"A Hot Property," by Ronald Wallace	"Junkyards," by Julian Lee Rayford	"Nothing Gold Can Stay," by Robert Frost
THEME															●				●	●
TONE				●	●															
SCENE		●					●		●					●		●				
STORY	●	●					●		●					●			●	●		
HYPERBOLE														●						
RHYME					●															●
ASSONANCE									●											
ALLITERATION						●						●								
SOUND					●	●			●		●	●								●
VOICE				●																
CHARACTER				●																
SIMILE	●	●						●												
PERSONIFICATION								●				●								
METAPHOR	●		●		●		●					●		●	●	●				
STANZA	●				●		●	●				●								
PLOT					●		●							●		●				
STRUCTURE					●	●	●	●		●	●	●	●			●	●	●	●	
LINE BREAKS		●						●	●			●		●						
MOOD	●	●			●							●								
PATTERNS								●					●							
REPETITION	●											●			●					
WORD CHOICE						●										●		●		
DETAILS	●		●				●	●			●									
IMAGE	●	●	●					●	●	●	●	●	●	●	●					

POEMS

souls. I like to think that we don't merely *read* a good poem; we experience it. Ted Hughes had that in mind when he wrote that poetry "is not made out of thoughts and casual fancies. It is made out of experiences which change our bodies, and spirits, whether momentarily or for good." I hope you will find that a poem in these pages is something that changes you.

I chose these poems because they seemed to be the right ones to serve as guides for the inexperienced reader of poetry. They are accessible and varied. You'll find poems about the city, poems about the country. Poems by people of color. Poems in various forms, rhyming and free verse. As guides, I trust them to assist readers on their way to a greater poetic literacy. I didn't choose "easy" or childish poems. "Easy" doesn't help a person/reader/writer grow. "Easy" leads to passive reception. I want students and their teachers to grow together in confidence and in their passion for poetry.

I want students to *reach* as they experience different poems. Reach when they encounter unfamiliar words or expressions. Reach when a poem offers a scene that is new to them. Reach when they experience a new feeling. To feel the growth and confidence that comes from exploring new territory. From exploration can come delight, excitement. Those delicious Oh-I-get-it moments that satisfy and encourage a reader to see, feel, hear what else is out there.

I see the journey of poetry in the classroom as a collaboration between teacher and student, as you open a poetic gift together. I'd like this book to be a part of that collaborative process. Teacher and student travel the path together but are not afraid to branch out in another direction, returning with a new poem to share, a wait-till-you-see-what-I-found poem. Teacher and student give and take, speak and listen, read and recite along a path to loving poetry. A path that takes your students and you beyond a poem, beyond your class, beyond this book to a passion that might include a book of poems on a night table, in a backpack, or in a locker, close at hand, ready to engage. A book of poems becomes a constant companion for a quiet moment without the intrusions of Facebook, MySpace, Skype, YouTube. Or, better yet, readers may create a quiet moment *for* a poem.

William Carlos Williams said that a poem is a "small (or large) machine made out of words." He went on to say, "When I say there's nothing sentimental about a poem, I mean that there can be no part that is redundant." I couldn't help but think of the time when my older brother took over the family garage to rebuild the 327-cubic-inch engine in his '67 Chevy. I can still see the parts carefully lined up on the workbench, still recall that intoxicating "garage smell" of gasoline and oil. We examined each part, and he explained its relationship to the other parts and to the engine itself. Each part—piston, camshaft, timing chain—had its role to play in making that engine purr and rumble but also roar when it needed to roar. And so it is with the parts of a poem. All the parts should make the poem purr, snarl, crackle, laugh, rumble, or roar.

What I've tried to do in this book is explore those parts of the poem. So, there will be talk about images and mood, line break and stanza, character and voice, and all manner of figurative language. But it all goes back to the words, doesn't it? Each word carefully chosen and placed in the right spot. Those parts of the machine that make it run. As Robert Francis observed, "One word cannot strike sparks from itself; it takes at least two for that. It takes words lying side by side to breed wonders." From those wonders comes a reader's joy. That's what I hope you and your students will discover: a passion for poetry as you experience the wonders that Francis describes. The world of poetry is a wonder-full place.

I trust you'll use this book in a way that best suits your needs and the needs of your students. Strictly speaking, the poems are not in any sequence, so you can jump around among the units without losing a sense of progression in the book. However, you might decide to start with Ted Kooser's haunting poem, "Abandoned Farmhouse" and work your way through all twenty units.

But before you decide how you want to use the book, I'd like you to read all the poems in it. I hope you find some of your favorites among them. I'm sure you'll meet some poets you recognize. See what the poets have to offer. Which poems do you like the most? Can you recognize how certain poems or terms fit into lessons you have already planned for your class? Perhaps you'll decide to use Janet S. Wong's poem for two voices, "Speak Up," when your students are reading a novel about racism or stereotyping. You might want to include "Friends in the Klan" by Marilyn Nelson or "Summertime Sharing" by Nikki Grimes during Black History Month. If you do skip around in the book, you may find a reference to a term or technique that I mentioned in one of the units you skipped. But that's a minor issue.

I encourage you to keep your own writer's notebook and write in it whenever your students are writing in theirs. It is the perfect way for you to make *Reading Poetry in the Middle Grades* your book. Beyond the underlining and margin jotting that I urge you to do in it, I hope that you use your writer's notebook as an extension of my book. You might want to divide your notebook into twenty sections, one for each unit in this book, and add to each section anything that will help you make the lesson a richer experience for your students. For each unit you can add new poems and online resources that compliment the material I offer. Perhaps a colleague will suggest a novel that relates well with a poem. Perhaps you've tweaked the writing suggestions. Or you had a brainstorm for an oral presentation of "Every Cat Has a Story." Write it all in your notebook and it will become invaluable.

I hope you encourage your students to be active readers of the poems. To read them with pen in hand, underlining parts of the poem that they like or that they find puzzling. Circling words that they enjoy. Using the margins to write questions to be raised during class discussion. To help students feel that they have room to comment on the poem or question parts of it, each poem is printed on a separate page, with lots of white space around it for note taking.

Below each poem is a box where students can jot down observations and questions about the poems. One of the first questions I always ask a class after they read a poem is, "What did you notice about the poem?" I suggest you ask your class the same question. The box below each poem is where they can write some answers to that question as they read each poem. Marking the poems and jotting down questions is a private matter for your students. I want them to feel that this box is their space. They can keep whatever they write there as private as they choose. Of course, my belief is that as they increase their confidence about their developing poetic literacy, they will be eager to share their questions and observations with the class.

Figure 3 illustrates how I marked the first poem in the book, "Abandoned Farmhouse" by Ted Kooser.

Figure 3

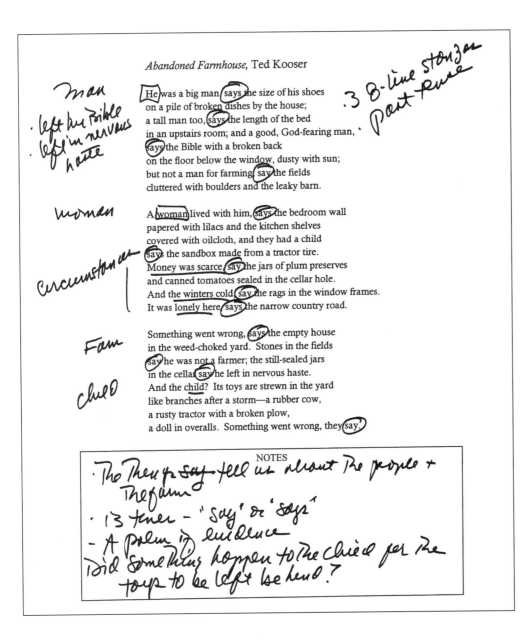

9

Obviously, neatness doesn't count, and it's important that your students understand that. This is where they can wonder and speculate. They might note the repetition of a word or a sound. They might notice a rhyme scheme. They might underline a few words that they need to look up in the dictionary. They can also use the space to ask questions about a poem, like "Why did the poet use this title? What does it have to do with the poem?" Or, "I *loved* the rhythm at the very end of the poem." Or, "I just don't get it. What's she talking about?"

When students interact with a poem in this way, they will be more likely to contribute to a class discussion about the poem. Their writing about a poem will be more solidly based on the text of the poem. I would encourage you to make a point of commenting when a student sees something in the poem that you hadn't noticed, saying something like, "I didn't notice that" or "I never thought of that." Also be aware of the *kinds* of things that your students notice and add them to your list of things that they might look for in other poems. Once something has been brought up by a student—say, punctuation in a poem—you can remind the class when they read the next poem to see if punctuation affects the way a poem reads. You can even post a list of such discoveries in the class as a reminder. Gradually, the class will build a substantial list of things to look for in a poem.

As you look though the book, you'll notice that each unit is organized in the same way.

- **BEFORE READING**—This section contains information about what makes the poem tick. Use this section to design a lesson with the featured poem that will engage your students.

  - **Why I Admire This Poem**—This brief introduction to the poem explains what attracted me to it.

  - **Companion Poems**—Here I mention a couple of other poems in the book that have qualities, such as a rural setting or engaging narrators, similar to the featured poem.

  - **Special Words to Work Through**—Because your students have various reading skills, it's important to point out any word play or vocabulary that they should be prepared for.

- **FIRST READING: Meeting the Poem**—In this section I give an introduction to the poem, exploring a few things to consider when you present it to your students.

- **CLOSE READING**—This section prepares you and the class for some of the things that they will be looking at in the poem. This introductory part is followed by a number of sections, specific guides that highlight terms and aspects of the poem that I hope you and your students will notice and discuss. These "noticing" sections will include things like mood, repetition, stanza, and figurative language—in other words, important parts of the machine.

- **AFTER READING**—This is an especially important part of each unit because it takes your students beyond the poem, showing them that a good poem is not merely something to "study" in class. Rather, it should contain truths and ideas that they can explore. The activities in this section are portals to a deeper exploration of each poem.

  - **Say It Out Loud**—A poem *must* be read aloud when it is a class assignment, of course, but also when students are reading poems for themselves. This section offers some suggestions for helping the students present each poem to an audience.

  - **Write About It**—The poems that I have included in this book will provoke your students to consider and discuss some of the issues that each poem raises. Beyond that, I want students to get in the habit of writing their reactions to poems as a way to better understand (and question) the poems and themselves. This section includes writing prompts to which the students can respond in their writer's notebook. Suggestions for writing poems and prose pieces are also included.

  - **Issues/Themes/Topics for Discussion**—In an attempt to link the poems to other aspects of your classroom discussion, I list a few ideas that you might make part of your class, such as bullying, poverty, and diversity.

  - **Book Bridges**—This section lists other books, fiction and nonfiction, that can be connected to the poems in some way.

  - **Online Resources**—You can also extend the lesson by using websites that are related to the poems.

Although this is a book about reading poetry, it is also a book about listening to poems. Over time, your students will become better listeners of poetry. They will hear the words and the feelings in a poem. They will hear the music of the words. And as Stanley Kunitz said, if we listen hard enough to poets, "who knows—we too may break into dance, perhaps for grief, perhaps for joy." I hope your classroom is filled with that dance.

Abandoned Farmhouse

Ted Kooser

He was a big man, says the size of his shoes
on a pile of broken dishes by the house;
a tall man too, says the length of the bed
in an upstairs room; and a good, God-fearing man,
says the Bible with a broken back
on the floor below the window, dusty with sun;
but not a man for farming, say the fields
cluttered with boulders and the leaky barn.

A woman lived with him, says the bedroom wall
papered with lilacs and the kitchen shelves
covered with oilcloth, and they had a child,
says the sandbox made from a tractor tire.
Money was scarce, say the jars of plum preserves
and canned tomatoes sealed in the cellar hole.
And the winters cold, say the rags in the window frames.
It was lonely here, says the narrow country road.

Something went wrong, says the empty house
in the weed-choked yard. Stones in the fields
say he was not a farmer; the still-sealed jars
in the cellar say she left in nervous haste.
And the child? Its toys are strewn in the yard
like branches after a storm—a rubber cow,
a rusty tractor with a broken plow,
a doll in overalls. Something went wrong, they say.

12

Notes ▶
Observations ▶
Questions ▶

▶ ABANDONED FARMHOUSE

Ted Kooser

■ BEFORE READING

Why I Admire This Poem

I have enjoyed Ted Kooser's poems for years. In fact, I included "Abandoned Farmhouse" in *Dont Forget to Fly*, an anthology I published over twenty-five years ago. Many of his poems tell a story (this poem contains the ghost of a story), and I like story poems. But what I find noteworthy about this poem is that he tells his story through things that are left behind in and around the derelict farmhouse. This in itself is a great lesson for young readers and writers: how the right details can tell a story.

In the first stanza, for example, we learn that the farmer was a *big man* from the *size of his shoes/on a pile of broken dishes*. We know from *the length of the bed/in an upstairs room* that he was a *tall man*. The farmer was a *good, God-fearing man*, according to *a Bible with a broken back/on the floor below the window*. He was, however, *not a man for farming*. So say *the fields/cluttered with boulders and the leaky barn*. And this is only the first stanza! As the story of the poem unfolds, we learn more about the family and the farm from other details.

Companion Poem

Consider this poem in conjunction with "Deserted Farm," by Mark Vinz, which also uses an abandoned farm as its setting. I find that Vinz's poem ends on a more hopeful note, which would be an interesting point of comparison to discuss with your class.

Special Words to Work Through

As you read the poem, do you find any words that might be difficult for your students? Perhaps *abandoned, scarce, boulders, oilcloth, strewn*? You may want to ask students to explain words that some members of the class might not be able to understand from the context and then write a couple of clarifying definitions on the board. When you are sure that the students understand these words, ask them if they can see any connection between the words. Most of the words—*abandoned, scarce, boulders, strewn*—contribute to the mood of desolation that is in the poem.

THEMES, ISSUES, CONCEPTS

• rural setting
• failure, loss
• poem of evidence
• success and failure

LITERARY TERMS

• images
• details
• mood
• repetition
• figurative language

ORGANIZERS

• Details
• Mood

13

FIRST READING: MEETING THE POEM

Before you distribute copies of the poem, divide your class into groups of two or three students and ask each group to select a couple of these questions to discuss:

- When you think of the "family farm," what images pop into your head?
- What are some of the good things about living on a farm?
- What personal qualities do you think would be important to survive as a farmer?
- What challenges might people on a farm face?
- What demands might farming put on a farm family?

Ask each group to report on their discussions. Write some of their findings on the board, where everyone can see them. After the class has read "Abandoned Farmhouse," they can compare and contrast their list to what they find in the poem.

Distribute copies of the poem and spend a few minutes explaining why it is important that the students read the poem actively, marking it and perhaps writing a few observations and questions about the poem. (See pages 8–10 for suggestions on how to help students become active readers.)

CLOSE READING: GETTING TO KNOW THE POEM

After students have read the poem—and this is something they can do at home if you want them to have time to let the poem sink in—ask questions, but refrain from supplying your take too fast. The conversation might unearth some of the following ideas.

This is a poem of failure. But it is also a poem of mystery. There is the ghost of a story here. We *know* the farm failed. It is, after all, abandoned. We know that the farmer *left in nervous haste.* What about his wife and child? Obviously, they're gone as well, but did they leave with him? Or could they have left without him? We *don't know* why the farm is abandoned. We'll never know why the farm failed, but we can find evidence that might shed some light on that mystery. The poet supplies that evidence in the details of the poem. (Figure 3, on page 9, lists some of the evidence I found in the poem.) We will not have all our questions answered, no matter how closely we read "Abandoned Farmhouse." And while that might be unsatisfactory for some readers, it's another reason I like the poem: those unanswered questions. Lingering questions offer readers something to continue thinking and wondering about.

Images

You might explore with students: Which details in the poem give you the clearest picture of a person or a scene? Which details help tell the story? Although we cannot physically *see* any people in the poem, the poet has noticed many specific things about them that may help us learn something about the characters as we read the poem. How do specific details, such as *the length of the bed*, help us picture the man? This poem asks the reader to go on a kind of archeologist's dig—to infer from the artifacts.

Distribute the **Details in "Abandoned Farmhouse"** organizer and ask the students to read the poem again, noting details about each character. I've included the farm/farmhouse on this sheet because, in a real way, the setting is a character that interacts with the other characters. You can carry this activity a step further by asking your students which sense they use with each detail. For example, they would use the sense of sight to *see the Bible with a broken back* or the sense of touch to *feel* the smooth oilcloth.

Noticing Mood

Beyond describing characters and telling a story, a poem often conveys a mood—somber or joyous, for example. As we read a poem, we frequently react to its mood. A poem with a joyous mood, for example, might lift our spirits.

How did your students feel after reading "Abandoned Farmhouse"? Were they moved by the empty farmhouse? Did they feel sorry for the family? Did they feel that the man wasn't qualified to be a farmer? That he should have known better than to try it? Can they point to specific words or phrases in the poem that contributed to this feeling?

Your students might also note that, tellingly, the word *broken* is repeated three times: the dishes are broken, the Bible has a broken back, and a toy tractor has a broken plow. Could the word *broken* also be used to describe the lives of the three people who lived in the farmhouse? What mood does the repetition of that word help create?

Distribute the **Mood in "Abandoned Farmhouse"** organizer which asks the students to put down in writing what many of them have felt and some of them have verbalized. The organizer asks them to record how they felt reading the poem and which words helped create that feeling.

Noticing Repetition

Did your students notice any words that were repeated a number of times in the poem? For instance, *say* or *says* is used thirteen times. (You might ask them to go back to the poem and underline or highlight every time these words are used. Marking the poem in this way will dramatize the importance of this small verb.) Why do they think Kooser used that word so often? Have them share their ideas. Such repetition does several things. First of all, repeating a word or a phrase stitches the poem together. Notice that the verb *say* is in the first and last lines, which act as bookends to contain the narrative. Indeed, *say* is the final word in the poem, providing a sense of closure. Also, this kind of repetition is one of the elements that gives a poem its rhythm. Repetition can mean the poet wants us to take special note.

Noticing Stanza

Many longer poems are divided into sections, or stanzas, of various numbers of lines. *Stanza* is an Italian word that means *room*, and just as walls divide one room from another, the extra space between groups of lines in a poem divides one group (stanza) from another. A stanza in a poem can be like a paragraph in prose writing; a new stanza introduces a new subject or moves the narrative arc of the poem a little further along.

Draw out students' ideas of how stanzas function. Next, ask whether they can see any reason Kooser grouped his lines the way he did. They may see that each stanza describes a character in his poem. We see the man in the opening stanza, the woman in the middle stanza, and the child in the final stanza. (The setting is described in all the stanzas and takes on the quality of a fourth character.)

You might want to use this discussion of structure as an introduction to having your students make an oral presentation of the poem. (See Say It Out Loud, below.)

Noticing Figurative Language

A *simile* is a comparison that uses *like* or *as*. Did your students notice how the poet uses a simile in the final stanza of the poem?

> And the child? Its toys are strewn in the yard
> like branches after a storm—

Poets use figurative language, as Kooser does here, to help the reader experience the poem more clearly. In this instance, the simile helps us *see* the scene more clearly than if the poet had written, *And the toys were all over the place.*

Generally, a simile is not as powerful as a metaphor, which is a direct comparison that does not use *like* or *as*. For example, *Juliet is an angel* (metaphor) is stronger writing than saying, *Juliet looks like an angel* (simile).

AFTER READING: KNOWING THE POEM FOREVER

Say It Out Loud

The students can perform this poem in numerous ways. Here are a few suggestions:

1. A chorus of a few voices can each read a stanza.

2. Two voices—one female, one male—can read the poem, reinforcing the pattern Kooser uses:

   Voice One: *He was a big man*

   Voice Two: *says the size of his shoes/on a pile of broken dishes by the house*

3. A single voice can read each stanza, perhaps a boy the first stanza, a girl the second, with the boy taking the first four lines of the final stanza, the girl the last four lines.

Can you see another way for your class to present the poem effectively? Ask the students for their own ideas about a performance. Give different boys and girls the chance to read sections of the poem so they can "try on" the emotions of both characters in the poem. Don't be afraid to experiment and ask the students to select the best interpretation and performance.

Write About It

Have students explore one of these ideas in their writer's notebook. Encourage them to try to feel the emotion that the characters are feeling.

1. Write a few journal/diary entries as if by one of the adults in the farmhouse.

2. Write a letter from the wife/mother to her parents or a sibling living in a distant city.

3. Assume the man or his wife has left a letter behind; what does it say?

4. Make a list of what you think your room and/or possessions say about you and your life. Model your list on the format that Kooser uses throughout the poem: *[He was] a tall man too, says the length of the bed/in an upstairs room.* Make sure that your list contains specific details, like the poem does.

5. Imitate the poet by rewriting several lines using your own ideas.

Issues/Themes/Topics for Discussion

- Farm life
- Homesteading
- Demise of the family farm
- Agribusiness
- What can make the difference between success and failure?

Related Poems

Ted Kooser has published about a dozen books of poems, many of which contain story poems of the plains, like "Abandoned Farmhouse." You might want to start with *Delights and Shadows*, a book about ordinary things made remarkable. Kooser's website, www.tedkooser.net, contains more information about his books.

Other poems to read:

"Farmhouse," by Leona Gom

"Old Farm in Northern Michigan," by Gary Gildner

Book Bridges

Finest Kind, by Lea Wait. When the crash of 1823 hits the United States, twelve-year-old Jake and his family leave Boston for the backwoods of Maine. Can they survive?

Little House on the Prairie, by Laura Ingalls Wilder. This title and several others in the series—*The Long Winter, Little Town on the Prairie, By the Shores of Silver Lake*—offer a vivid picture of life on the prairie in the mid-1880s.

The Borning Room by Paul Fleischman. Nearing the end of her life, Georgiana recalls her life and all its triumphs and tragedies. Each scene is connected to the room in which she now lies.

Time to Go by Beverly and David Fiday. This picture book, illustrated by Thomas B. Allen, tells the story of children who must be separated from the farm on which they grew up. But times are tough, and the family must move on.

Online Resources

- www.americanlifeinpoetry.org, which Kooser set up when he was the poet laureate of the United States, contains many accessible poems.

- To give your students more information about living on the prairie in the mid-1800s, visit the website of the Illinois State Museum and explore "At Home on the Fringe of the Prairie 1800–1850"—www.museum.state.il.us/exhibits/athome/1800/welcome.htm.

Name _____ Date _____ Class_____

Details in "Abandoned Farmhouse" _____

In the columns below, jot down details from the poem that tell you something about the characters in the poem.

man	woman	child	farm/farmhouse

Mood in "Abandoned Farmhouse"

In each box on the left, write down a way you felt as you read the poem. On the lines to the right, write down some words and phrases that contributed to that feeling.

Deserted Farm

Mark Vinz

Where the barn stood
the empty milking stalls rise up
like the skeleton of an ancient sea beast,
exiled forever on shores of prairie.

Decaying timber moans softly in twilight;
the house collapses like a broken prayer.
Tomorrow the heavy lilac blossoms will open,
higher than the roofbeams, reeling in wind.

Notes ▶
Observations ▶
Questions ▶

From *Reading Poetry in the Middle Grades*. Portsmouth, NH: Heinemann. © 1975 by Mark Vinz from *Winter Promises*, published by Book Market Press. Reprinted by permission of the author.

▶ DESERTED FARM

Mark Vinz

BEFORE READING

Why I Admire This Poem

Mark Vinz is another of those "prairie poets" I seem to be drawn to. He captures in "Deserted Farm" the same desolation that Kooser catches in "Abandoned Farmhouse." However, there is a difference between the poems. Whereas Kooser obliquely tells a story, Vinz is more concerned with painting a scene. There is of course a story behind his deserted farm—there is often a story in a poem if we look closely enough—but Vinz isn't interested in telling that story. He simply wants to paint a picture with his words—which is not to minimize this poem or what it took to write it. Mark Vinz packs his eight-line poem with comparisons—via metaphor, simile, and personification—that make it incredibly rich.

Companion Poem

Consider this poem in conjunction with "Abandoned Farmhouse," because they are both poems of the prairie. Neither poem has any people in it, although Kooser tells of people who lived on the farm at one time. What reactions do your students have to both poems?

Special Words to Work Through

As you read the poem, do any words seem difficult for your students, perhaps *exiled, prairie, decaying, collapses, lilac*? They may or may not be familiar with the two meanings of *reeling*, as well (I have more to say about that word later). If there are words that they will not be able to understand from the context, write a couple of clarifying definitions on the board.

Is the adjective in this poem's title a synonym for the adjective in "Abandoned Farmhouse"? Both connote emptiness, yet *abandoned* means that someone has left a place or an object, while *deserted* may mean simply that there is no one there. As we read both poems, we see that these adjectives are, indeed, apt. We learn that people have left the farmhouse in Kooser's poem, whereas Vinz describes derelict buildings.

THEMES, ISSUES, CONCEPTS

- loss
- hope
- change

LITERARY TERMS

- line break
- mood
- simile

ORGANIZERS

- Line Break
- Scene

23

FIRST READING: MEETING THE POEM

"Deserted Farm" is a poem of place. Vinz creates a scene with his words and images. In a sense, it is also a poem of contrast. Vinz describes what's left of two structures, but readers must contrast a mental image of the house and barn intact with the picture Vinz creates. Only if we have an image of how large and majestic the barn once was, how solid and foursquare the house, will we get the full impact of his poem.

After your students have read the poem, hand out the **Scene in "Deserted Farm"** organizer—which is a blank sheet of paper with a frame around the edge. Call attention to the small "plaque" on the bottom of the frame—*Deserted Farm*, by Mark Vinz—and ask your students to draw the scene they imagine after reading the poem. Students who have as little talent for drawing as I do may panic. Reassure them that their "work of art" will not be graded. The purpose of having them draw the scene is to see whether they can include the main elements that Vinz describes. If your students have no idea what a farm or a barn looks like, share a picture downloaded from one of the resource websites.

CLOSE READING: GETTING TO KNOW THE POEM

"Deserted Farm" is a poem of loss, but it is also a poem about change, about hope. It is a poem about looking to the future, even though the first six lines convey a mood of desolation. First, the title tells us that the farm is deserted, vacant. *Where the barn stood* tells us that it doesn't stand there any more. The milking stalls are empty and *rise up/like the skeleton of an ancient sea beast*. I like his use of *exiled forever*, which connotes something forsaken, never to be returned to. Vinz adds to the mood of desolation when he personifies the *decaying timber* as moaning softly. What's more, the house has fallen in *like a broken prayer*. All in all, a pretty bleak picture, but, unlike Kooser, he includes no specific remnants of the people who used to live there.

But the bleak picture, which ends with a period at the end of line 6, turns suddenly hopeful when line 7 begins with *Tomorrow* and goes on to describe the *heavy lilac blossoms . . . higher than the roofbeams* that are about to open, bringing with them all the glorious color and life of spring. The poem turns on a dime, going from desolation to riotous *reeling* blossoms. Even on this deserted farm, there will continue to be life.

I also love how Vinz takes advantage of two meanings of *reeling*. That word shows the huge bush swaying in the wind, but it also evokes the action of a fisherman swaying back and forth as he reels in a big catch.

Noticing Line Breaks

How do poets know what words go on a line? Why do they break their lines where they do? Line breaks can be one of the most difficult concepts for inexperienced poetry readers (and writers) to grasp. Kids find a certain security in rhyming lines of poetry of roughly the same length. Free verse—which is free of any set or predicable rhythm, rhyme, or line length—often confuses them. *It looks like the poet ended the lines wherever he wanted to! Why did he put just* these *words on a line?* Luckily, "Deserted Farm" is a good example of a free verse poem with logical line breaks.

Free verse poets try to put on each line words that go together, words that make sense together. That's not to say that a line needs to be a complete thought, as in a sentence. Sensible line breaks make the poem easier to read, easier to understand. Sloppy line breaks confuse a reader. When there is no punctuation at the end of a line, it should lead into the next line with an ever-so-slight pause, "half a comma" as someone has said. *Enjambment* is the term describing a line of poetry that continues into the following line.

To help your students get a handle on line breaks in free verse, give them the "prose" version of my poem "Stories" (see handout). None of the words or punctuation has been changed; the only difference is that it looks like a paragraph instead of a poem. Have students, in pairs, read the passage, decide which words sound like they "go together," and draw slashes in the text to indicate where one group of words ends and the next one begins. Once they have decided which words make sense together, have them write each group of words on a different line so it looks like a poem. Chances are, most of the versions students create will be very close to the real poem (also a handout). This exercise bears repeating from time to time with other poems. It encourages students to look carefully at the words that a poet puts on a line.

When your students look closely at the line breaks in "Deserted Farm," they will discover that Vinz has broken his lines into logical groups of words. Ask a student to read "Deserted Farm" aloud, stopping just long enough at the end of each line so the class has time to note how the words on each line make sense together. You wouldn't expect Vinz to write a line like *Where the barn stood the empty* or *milking stalls rise up like the.* The last two words of both of these "lines" just don't belong with the other words. In fact, they distract us from the other words in the lines. Also bear in mind that a line may hold but a single word, if the poet wants to emphasize that word.

Noticing Mood

After the students have heard "Deserted Farm" read aloud a few times, ask them to mark off words in the poem that catch their attention. Write the words and phrases they notice—most likely *empty, skeleton, exiled forever, decaying, moans, collapses, broken*—on the board. Ask whether the words have anything in common. Some of your kids will notice the somber mood these words create.

Do students mention how the mood of the poem changes with *Tomorrow* at the beginning of line 7? That's the turning point of the poem. The scene in the final two lines is brighter and more hopeful. The poem ends with a delicious scene of the lilacs *reeling in wind.*

Noticing Figurative Language

Mark Vinz uses two strong similes in his poem: *the empty milking stalls rise up/like the skeleton of an ancient sea beast* and *the house collapses like a broken prayer*. Ask your students what they see in the comparisons. The first one is a visual simile. We can see the skeleton. The second simile is a bit more complicated. It gives us a *feeling* more than a visual image. What do your students think when they read the words *broken prayer*? For me that phrase connotes the rejection of an unanswered prayer, but your students might have a different take on it.

A number of the words in the poem refer to the sea. In the first stanza, Vinz uses sea-related terms to show size. He shows the size of the milking stalls by comparing the timbers to *the skeleton of an ancient sea beast*. Then, to show how vast the prairie is, he uses the metaphor *shores of prairie*. And we have already talked about two different meanings of "reeling," one of which refers to fishing.

AFTER READING: KNOWING THE POEM FOREVER

Say It Out Loud

After your class has had a chance to discuss the tone of this poem, with its shift in the final two lines, ask them whether this gives them any ideas on how to perform the poem. Perhaps the first six lines of the poem will be read by a group of somber, masculine voices, the final two lines by girls.

Write About It

Have students explore one of these ideas in their writer's notebook:

1. Write about a change or loss you have experienced and how it affected your life. It could be losing a crucial ball game or the death of a friend or relative.

2. Change can bring opportunities as well as setbacks. Moving to a new city, for example, can bring exciting new surroundings and new friends but also the sadness of leaving old friends and comfortable surroundings. Write about some of the opportunities that have come to you because of a change.

3. Can you think of a change you would like to see in yourself or in your family or at school? If you would like to change something about yourself, what's stopping you? What are the obstacles you face?

Issues/Themes/Topics for Discussion

- Changes in science: the seasons, ecosystems, and so on
- Changes in farming that have been brought on by the growth of agribusiness

- Hope
- Loss

Related Poems

"The Hermitage," by Bill Dodd

"Eldora in July," by Tom Clark

"Cannon Hill," by Sandra Hochman

Book Bridges

Out of the Dust, by Karen Hess. In this novel in verse, Hess captures all the uncertainties and hardships of families caught in the Dust Bowl of the 1930s.

Online Resources

You can find pictures of barns at these sites:

- www.readthehook.com/kids/wp-content/uploads/2009/03/ivy-creek-barn.jpg
- www.littlebournebarn.co.uk/images/Littleborne%20Barn%20Interior.JPG
- Garrison Keillor's The Writer's Almanac website, writersalmanac.publicradio.org, contains two Mark Vinz poems. (Bookmark this site; it contains many accessible poems.)

There's another Mark Vinz poem at

- www.americanlifeinpoetry.org/columns/229.html (another site that deserves a "fabulous poetry" bookmark).

Name _____ Date _____ Class _____

Scene in "Deserted Farm"

"Deserted Farm" by Mark Vinz

Name _____ Date _____ Class _____

Stories

Old Lester Darby, thin as a wire, sat at a card table, retirement pocket watch ticking next to a half-completed jigsaw puzzle of Mount Rushmore, and told hours of stories about baseball and the days he played with the St. Louis Browns, back, as he said, when players weren't a bunch of sissies, about fanning Ruth and Gehrig in '28, about long smoky train rides in sleeper cars, about ladies who loved pitchers. Until Raymond looked him up in the *Baseball Encyclopedia* in the library and found nothing. When we went to ask him why he did it, Lester Darby, waiting with lemonade on the porch as the sun slid home, said, "Did I ever tell you about the time I got in a fist fight with Ty Cobb in a hotel in Detroit?" And we decided the stories were better than the truth.

Name _____ Date _____ Class _____

Stories

Old Lester Darby,
thin as wire,
sat at a card table,
retirement pocket watch ticking
next to a half-completed
jigsaw puzzle of Mount Rushmore,
and told hours of stories about baseball
and the days he played
with the St. Louis Browns,
back, as he said, when
players weren't a bunch of sissies,
about fanning Ruth and Gehrig in '28,
about long smoky train rides in sleeper cars,
about ladies who loved pitchers.
Until Raymond looked him up
in the *Baseball Encyclopedia*
in the library and found nothing.
When we went to ask him
why he did it,
Lester Darby,
waiting with lemonade on the porch
as the sun slid home,
said, "Did I ever tell you about the time
I got in a fist fight with Ty Cobb
in a hotel in Detroit?'
And we decided the stories
were better than the truth.

When It Is Snowing

Siv Cedering

When it is snowing
the blue jay
is the only piece of
sky
in my backyard.

Poppies

Roy Scheele

The light in them stands as clear as water
drawn from a well.
When the breeze moves across them they totter.
You half expect them to spill.

32

Notes ▶

Observations ▶

Questions ▶

"When It Is Snowing"

"Poppies"

From *Reading Poetry in the Middle Grades*. Portsmouth, NH: Heinemann. "When It Is Snowing" © 1977 by Siv Cedering from *The Juggler*, published by Sagarin Press. Reprinted by permission of the Estate of Siv Cedering. "Poppies" © 1979 by Roy Scheele from *Noticing*, published by Three Sheets Press. Reprinted by permission of the author.

▶ **WHEN IT IS SNOWING / POPPIES**

Siv Cedering / Roy Scheele

BEFORE READING

Why I Admire These Poems

For a number of reasons, short poems are often my favorites. For one thing, I admire a poet who can create a striking image with a handful or two of words. Also, students are often less intimidated by short poems. Good short poems show students that a poem need not be long and complicated, built on layers of meaning. I've found that young writers are more apt to write a poem if they see that it can be short. They see how "When It Is Snowing" and "Poppies" each create one clear image. And that is all a poem *needs* to do, isn't it? Create one strong image?

I often use short poems in tandem because there might not be enough in one short poem to sustain a discussion. On the other hand, a pair of short poems can offer points of comparison and contrast. These two poems can help students see how important it is to pay attention if they want to write a good poem. These short poems focus on very limited scenes.

Companion Poem

I like to use short imagistic poems like these with Naomi Shihab Nye's "Every Cat Has a Story" because that poem is also built of short imagistic stanzas that each create one striking image appealing to one of the senses.

Special Words to Work Through

The vocabulary in these poems is pretty simple, although *totter*—a great word, don't you think!—in "Poppies" may be a new word for some of your students. It's important that they understand the meaning of *totter* because it is integral to the image that Scheele creates. Likewise, it's important that your students know what a poppy looks like. Go to http://en.wikipedia.org/wiki/Poppy to find some good photos of poppies.

FIRST READING: MEETING THE POEMS

What do your students expect to find in a good poem? As discussion develops, write their answers on the board or on chart paper. Chances are they'll offer poetic qualities like rhyme and rhythm. Some will no doubt feel that a poem needs to contain

THEMES, ISSUES, CONCEPTS

- writer's notebook
- paying attention

LITERARY TERMS

- images
- metaphor

ORGANIZERS

- Details and Senses

33

a "message." This notion comes from the mistaken belief that writing a poem requires more than creating an image with clear and vivid language. For some students, the image is not enough.

While it's true that poems often have layers of meaning, they need not deliver a "message" to the reader. A story is told of a famous Hollywood producer who told a screenwriter, "If you want to send a message, call Western Union." I think you can say the same for poetry. Resist the urge to find a "moral" in a poem. Let the poem speak to you and your students. Rely on a class discussion that allows students to raise issues they find in the poem.

Save your students' suggestions of qualities to expect in a good poem, and tell the class that as you read and explore more poems together, you will add to this list. Eventually, it will include things like image, sense details, figurative language, and various elements of sound.

CLOSE READING: GETTING TO KNOW THE POEMS

Reading these poems provides a good opportunity to talk to the class about the value of keeping a writer's notebook, a place where they can jot down observations, details, and comparisons—things they notice. In a sense, the writer's notebook is like a science lab where they can experiment with language. It's a locker where they can jam and store all manner of observations. They can make lists of words, write drafts of poems, compose love letters they'll never send, move words around. Anything goes and nothing is "wrong" with anything they write. This is one of the reasons my writer's notebook is one of my favorite places to go.

What things might your students include in their writer's notebook? Well, you could give them some time to observe. What should they observe? *Whatever they want!* That sounds glib, but that's really what the notebook is for. In this case, I would send them out to look carefully at small scenes or small things, as Nye did with her cats and Scheele did with his poppies. Do they notice something in their neighborhood, like a neon sign that is only partly lit, a page of a newspaper caught on a chainlink fence, or a flag snapping in the breeze? Have they been drawn to a shaft of early morning sunlight, had street noises wake them in the middle of the night, or watched raindrops sliding down the classroom window? In some of these examples, I name things you can hear and feel, but make sure your students understand that they need to be open to what may come to them through all their senses.

Remind the class that in addition to being an opportunity for them to pay attention, close observation is also a chance for them to be patient. There is no need to rush. They might spend a week observing things outside and inside, in their neighborhood, in their school, in their home, looking and listening for details.

Remind them how Cedering and Scheele built their poems around small details. Can they fashion some of their own detailed observations into a poem? Their poem need not be long. But it *must* be built on a clear image that appeals to one of the senses.

Noticing Images

Of course, a good poem often does more than create an image that resonates with the reader, but the image is the core of a good poem—the foundation. (As you read the poems in this book, as well as other good poems, you'll see what I mean.) I'm a bit reluctant to use the word *image* in this context, because it connotes something visual, and a poem can appeal to other senses as well. The images in these two poems, however, do rely on the sense of sight.

Distribute the **Details and Senses** organizer and ask the students to read both poems again, using the column headed *Details* to list the details they noticed in the poem, and noting in the next column the sense each detail appeals to.

The students will discover that both poems use details that appeal to the sense of sight. Notice that Cedering uses details—*snowing, blue jay, sky*—that you can see, especially color. Yes, you can feel how cold and wet snow is, and you can hear a blue jay squawk, but the poet is concerned only with what she sees. Scheele also concentrates on what he can see: *light, clear as water.* Further, he compares the poppies to a container, like a cup, and says, *When the breeze moves across them they totter/You half expect them to spill*, creating the visual image of the breeze making the flowers unsteady.

Noticing Figurative Language

How do these poets create their images? Did your class notice how Roy Scheele makes a comparison between the poppy and a container that holds water? He doesn't write a simile—a comparison using *like* or *as*; he doesn't say that the flower is *like* a cup. Nor does he say that the flower *is* a cup, which would be metaphor. Rather, he describes what he sees and a *reader* makes that comparison when she reads the poem.

Siv Cedering uses a *metaphor* in her poem when she says that *the blue jay/is the only piece of/sky*. It's a visual metaphor since it compares the color of the bird and the color of the sky on a bright day. The metaphor is even more striking, I think, because of the contrast with the snow. There is no blue sky on that snowy day, except in the blue of the blue jay.

Metaphors offer a wonderful opportunity for readers to go beyond the apparent meaning of the words and to infer what the poet is saying. In this case, what is Cedering hoping the reader will infer from *the blue jay/is the only piece of/sky*?

35

AFTER READING: KNOWING THE POEMS FOREVER

Say It Out Loud

Although both poems are short, they *read* differently, and the only way to hear the difference is by reading them out loud. Ask a couple of students (both boys and girls) to read the poems aloud individually. Do your students notice anything about the poems as they hear them? Does one poem sound smoother than the other?

Do any of your students notice the rhymes in Scheele's poem? They're not exact rhymes like *cat/hat*, but they're rhymes nonetheless: *water/totter, well/spill*. This kind of rhyme goes by many names, for example, half rhyme and slant rhyme.

Do you get a different feel from Scheele's longer rhyming lines than you get from Cedering's short lines?

Write About It

Have students explore one of these ideas using their writer's notebook:

1. Look through your writer's notebook and see whether you've captured some details and images that you can fashion into a short free verse poem. You can also string together a series of related short stanzas to build a poem as Naomi Shihab Nye did in "Every Cat Has a Story."

2. Get together with a writing partner and share some of the things that you've collected in your writer's notebook. You might be able to swap images. Or, something your partner wrote may give you an idea for a piece of writing.

Issues/Themes/Topics of Discussion

- What are some good places in which to observe people?
- Where is your favorite place to observe nature? Your neighborhood?
- Share one of your favorite observations.

Related Poems

"Apple," by Nan Fry

"Snow Fence," by Ted Kooser

"About an Excavation," by Charles Reznikoff

"The City," by David Ignatow

"The Moon Was But a Chin of Gold," by Emily Dickinson

Online Resources

- When he's not writing poems, Roy Scheele teaches at Doane College, in Crete, Nebraska, where he is poet in residence. The website www.futurecycle.org/RoyScheeleBio.aspx contains information about him, as well as a couple of poems from his recent books. In addition, his poem "Planting a Dogwood" can be found on the American Life in Poetry site: www.americanlifeinpoetry.org/columns/073.html.

- Siv Cedering (1939–2007) was a multidimensional artist. Not only did she write poems for children and adults, she was also a prolific translator, composer, and visual artist. Her website—www.cedering.com—shows the breadth of her work. Make sure you check out the samples of her paintings and sculptors. Many of them are wild, in contrast to many of her poems. The site www.poets.org/poet.php/prmPID/190 also provides some information about Cedering, as well as a link to her poem "Hands."

Name _____ Date _____ Class _____

Details and Senses in "When It Is Snowing" and "Poppies"

Poem	Details	Sense Appealed To
"When It Is Snowing"		
"Poppies"		

Speak Up

Janet S. Wong

You're Korean, aren't you?

    Yes.

Why don't you speak
Korean?

    Just don't, I guess.

Say something Korean.

    I don't speak it.
    I can't.

C'mon. Say something.

    Halmoni. Grandmother.
    Haraboji. Grandfather.
    Imo. Aunt.

Say some other stuff.
Sounds funny.
Sounds strange.

    Hey, let's listen to you
    for a change.

Listen to me?

    Say some foreign words.

But I'm American,
can't you see?

    Your family came from
    somewhere else.
    Sometime.

But I was born here.

    So was I.

40

Notes ▶
Observations ▶
Questions ▶

Janet S. Wong

BEFORE READING

Why I Admire This Poem

"Speak Up" is a skillful marriage of form and function. Rather than merely preach about what it means to be an "American," Janet S. Wong uses dialogue to show two different attitudes toward this explosive issue. Just as the dialogue in a play or movie shows character, Wong accomplishes the same feat in her poem. The tension be- tween the two speakers is apparent right from the opening line, "*You're Korean, aren't you?*" Sounds like an accusation, don't you think? The tension builds from there as the two speakers continue their dialogue.

Some historians believe that poems for different voices originated in sixteenth- century churches with choral readings. At any rate, poems in two voices came into their own with the publication of *Joyful Noise*, by Paul Fleischman, in 1988. The poem in two voices is a challenging form to write and to read, because it often includes lines that are spoken simultaneously as well as those that are spoken in response to other lines. (To make the discussion here less cumbersome, I will refer to the person who says the lines in the left column as speaker 1 and *he*. The other speaker is speaker 2 and *she*. I'm making no gender assumptions with this decision.)

Companion Poem

Consider this poem in conjunction with "Friends in the Klan," by Marilyn Nelson, because the two poems show degrees of intolerance. What causes the intolerance of speaker 1 in Wong's poem to grow into the intolerance of the "friend" who sends the anonymous threatening letter to Dr. Carver in Nelson's poem?

Special Words to Work Through

There are probably no words in this poem that your students will not understand. However, unless they are Korean, they will need help pronouncing the Korean words for *grandmother, grandfather,* and *aunt: halmoni, haraboji,* and *imo*. Write the phonetic pronunciations on the board so the students can see them as they read the poem:

> *halmoni* (grandmother): HAHL mō nē
>
> *haraboji* (grandfather): HAH rah bō jē
>
> *imo* (aunt): EE mō

THEMES, ISSUES, CONCEPTS

- Asian American poet
- being an "American"
- tension in a poem
- immigration
- stereotypes
- racism

LITERARY TERMS

- tone
- character
- poem in two voices

ORGANIZERS

- Family Tree
- Character

41

You might also point out how speaker 1 in the poem is given to labeling. He uses *Korean* three times in a way that shows he feels the girl is different, someone less than a true "American." He continues this attitude later in the poem when he declares "*I'm an American,*" again using a label to indicate a difference between him and speaker 2. This label, however, shows a superiority that is missing when he uses *Korean* the first three times he speaks in the poem.

FIRST READING: **MEETING THE POEM**

What does it mean to be an "American"? Ask your class for their answers to that question. Students might offer the names of people they consider to be Americans. List their replies on the board. Can they see any common ground in their responses? Can they agree on five or six qualities? Ask your class how an American acts. What does an American look like? What does he/she sound like? Are there things that "disqualify" you from being an American?

You can carry this activity a bit further by suggesting the names of Americans of various beliefs, backgrounds, and convictions (athletes, movie stars, talk show hosts) to see how they stack up against the class criteria. You might suggest people such as Cesar Chavez, who, with an eighth-grade education, used nonviolent methods to fight for the rights of migrant farm workers. Or Rosa Parks, a department store worker who refused to move to the back of the bus where the black riders "belonged." Or Clara Breed (www.janm.org/collections/clara-breed-collection), a children's librarian in San Diego who became a friend and advocate for the thousands of Japanese American children confined to internment camps during World War II.

I'd like kids to realize that the "true American" is not only the person who waves the flag or spouts the Bill of Rights. Americans are citizens who act on behalf of their country, serving other, often less fortunate, citizens.

Before reading the poem, distribute copies of the **Family Tree** organizer, a simplified family tree with spaces for students to enter the names of their parents, grandparents, and great-grandparents. Some students will have trouble going back that far, but the assignment will prompt them to talk to their parents and other relatives about their ancestors and discover stories about them. They may be surprised by what they hear. Encourage them to record some of these "oral histories."

When the students have filled in as much of their family tree as they can, the class can discuss the question, "How American are you?" Information in the Online Resources section will help you deepen these explorations of students' (and your) heritage.

CLOSE READING: GETTING TO KNOW THE POEM

One thing this poem in two voices does is show tension in relatively few words, starting with the opening line, "*You're Korean, aren't you?*" Speaker 1 continues to badger speaker 2, whose simple replies exasperate him. When he asks, "*Why don't you speak/Korean?*" speaker 2's reply is equally brief: "*Just don't, I guess.*" Speaker 1 shoots back a command, "*Say something Korean,*" then in his next line, "*C'mon. Say something.*" When speaker 2 replies with a few rudimentary Korean words, he isn't satisfied and demands that she "*say some other stuff.*" He ratchets up the tension when he demeans what she said: "*Sounds funny./Sounds strange.*" The poem changes at this point, when speaker 2 retorts, "*Hey, let's listen to you/for a change.*" From there to the end of the poem, she turns the tables on her antagonist, trying to get him to see that we all come from "*somewhere else./Sometime.*"

Ask your students to consider how Wong creates a dramatic situation with two characters in relatively few words. Economy of language is one of the qualities that distinguishes poetry from prose. Done skillfully, it is also one of the things that gives poetry its power.

Noticing Tone

Reading the poem out loud with another person is the best way to catch the tone of the characters, especially speaker 1, who exudes an attitude of superiority, using the word *Korean* in each of his first three lines in a manner that is clearly condescending. In addition, he is demanding—"*Say something Korean. . . . C'mon. Say something. . . . Say some other stuff*"—as if she needs to perform for him. He also judges her, calling her Korean words "*funny . . . strange.*"

In counterpoint, speaker 2's tone is quiet and reasonable, even accommodating in the first half of the poem. Then she becomes fed up with his arrogance and says, "*Hey, let's listen to you/for a change.*" From then on, his tone becomes more defensive the more she asserts herself.

You may want to introduce the Say It Out Loud part of the lesson (see next page) now rather than wait until later.

Noticing Character

What did your students picture when they read the poem and listened to it being read aloud? Not physically, of course, because there is no evidence about what either speaker looks like—but what about their character? How would they describe each speaker's character? How did your students come up with their pictures of the speakers? In other words, what details did they pick up by what the characters say and how they say it? The **Character** organizer may help your students organize their thoughts and gather evidence.

One way to get a better sense of the character of each of the speakers is to read what speaker 1 says from beginning to end, then read the lines of speaker 2 from start to finish. Ask two students in your class to do just that. Without the change from one character to another, the tone that each character uses is more apparent. After several pairs of students have read the poem in this way, revisit the completed **Character** organizer. Ask whether hearing the poem read in this way changes their opinion of each character.

Noticing the Two Voices

The poem in two voices is a back-and-forth form. It consists of dialogue between two speakers. In this poem the speakers are persons, but the two voices can be animals or insects, as Paul Fleischman showed in his ground-breaking collection, *Joyful Noise*.

One way Wong keeps the dialogue going in "Speak Up" is to have speaker 1 ask questions or give commands, to which speaker 2 responds. Your students may have noticed that of the first five lines spoken by speaker 1, two are questions and three are commands. The tone of each speaker changes when speaker 2 challenges speaker 1 and makes a demand of her own, "*Hey, let's listen to you.*" His next two lines are rhetorical questions: "*Listen to me?*" and "*But I'm an American,/can't you see?*" Using questions and commands allows the poet to maintain the back-and-forth flow.

AFTER READING: KNOWING THE POEM FOREVER

Say It Out Loud

With practice your students will be able to master presenting the poem orally. But it takes patience, because readers need to let the other person get a chance to say his/her lines.

Before you choose teams to present the poem, ask your students to read it through to themselves a couple of times. Although there is no gender given for either of the speakers in the poem, my guess is that most of your students will think that the first speaker is a boy and the second is a girl. Or will they? Does one of the speakers "sound more like a boy"? Why? As you choose students to present this poem, be sure to include all the possible combinations of girls and boys, because this may affect the way the poem is experienced. For example, would the poem sound different if the two speakers were boys? Or girls? How about if the more aggressive speaker were a girl? While the poem explores racial stereotypes, it offers a chance for your class to discuss gender stereotypes as well.

Write About It

Have students explore one of these ideas in their writer's notebook:

1. Write about a time when you were insensitive to someone who was "different." How was that person "different" in your eyes? Or perhaps it was a time when you witnessed such treatment. Or was there a time when *you* were on the receiving end of insensitivity because you were "different"? Consider why you were perceived as "different" in that situation.

2. What should the United States' immigration policy be? Let everyone in (we are, after all, "the melting pot")? Send all the "foreigners" back to where they came from so they stop taking American jobs? You might write a letter to one of the senators from your state and share your views on immigration policy. You can find your senator's mailing address here: www.congressmerge.com/onlinedb/

3. "Speak Up" poses an interesting question: just what *does* make someone an American? Is it something you can see? Is it about where you were born? Is it about where your ancestors came from? Is it about what you can contribute to your country?

4. Does speaker 2 want to be invisible in a way? Have you ever wanted to be invisible? Why? You can write about that time and how you coped with the situation.

Issues/Themes/Topics for Discussion

*   Immigration/immigrants
*   Ellis Island
*   Diversity
*   Gender stereotypes
*   Racial stereotypes

Research

Have students research how many words we consider "American" are really borrowed from other languages. The number of words that have come into the English language from other cultures is staggering. Here is a short list:

*   Dutch: *brick, pinky, batik, brawl*
*   French: *boutique, buffet, fiancé, rendezvous*
*   German: *kindergarten, aspirin, cobalt, diesel, glitz*
*   Spanish: *barbecue, anchovy, breeze, jade*
*   Greek: *acoustic, delta, arithmetic, icon*

Book Bridges

Good collections of poems for two voices, beginning with the one that got everyone talking about this genre:

Joyful Noise: Poems for Two Voices, by Paul Fleischman.

I Am Phoenix: Poems for Two Voices, by Paul Fleischman.

Math Talk: Mathematical Ideas in Poems for Two Voices, by Theoni Pappas.

Messing Around on the Monkey Bars and Other School Poems for Two Voices, by Betsy Franco.

You can find some poems about identity suitable for younger readers in *Hey World, Here I Am!* by Jean Little.

Novels about racial stereotyping:

Cooper's Lesson, by Sun Yung Shin, illustrated by Kim Cogan, translated by Min Paek. A picture book about a biracial Korean American boy who feels uncomfortable trying to speak Korean.

Project Mulberry, by Lind Sue Park. An after-school project on silk worms leads the Korean American protagonist and her friend to learn about tolerance, prejudice, and friendship.

Slant, by Laura E. Williams. The thirteen-year-old protagonist, tired of being called "slant," considers plastic surgery as a solution to her feelings.

Online Resources

Oral history links:

- For a good step-by-step guide to "doing" oral history, go to http://dohistory.org/on_your_own/toolkit/oralHistory.html.

- History Matters calls itself "The U.S. Survey Course on the Web"; the site includes a good exploration of "oral history"—go to http://historymatters.gmu.edu/mse/oral/what.html.

Ancestry links:

Tracing ancestry can be confusing and time-consuming. Nonetheless, here are a couple of sites that can offer some good advice:

- www.infoplease.com/spot/genealogy1.html offers a basic genealogy guide.

- One of the foremost online ancestry sites is www.ancestry.com. Although it is a subscription site, it does offer some basic information without charge.

Immigration links:

- Students whose ancestors arrived in the United States through Ellis Island might enjoy researching some passenger lists for ships that entered the Port of New York from 1892–1924. They can find these records at www.ellisisland.org. It is a great site to browse.

- Asian American students might be interested in checking out www.asiannation.org/first.shtml, which deals with Asian American history, demographics, and related issues.

Name _____ Date _____ Class _____

Family Tree

paternal great-grandfather	paternal great-grandmother	paternal great-grandfather	paternal great-grandmother	maternal great-grandfather	maternal great-grandmother	maternal great-grandfather	maternal great-grandmother

paternal grandfather	paternal grandmother	maternal grandfather	maternal grandmother

father	mother

notes

© 2011 by Paul B. Janeczko from *Reading Poetry in the Middle Grades*. Portsmouth, NH: Heinemann.

Name _____ Date _____ Class _____

Character in "Speak Up"

Character 1	Character 2
Qualities	**Qualities**
Evidence, Details	**Evidence, Details**

A POISON TREE

William Blake

I was angry with my friend:
I told my wrath, my wrath did end.
I was angry with my foe:
I told it not, my wrath did grow.

And I water'd it in fears,
Night and morning with my tears;
And I sunned it with my smiles
And with soft deceitful wiles.

And it grew both day and night,
Till it bore an apple bright;
And my foe beheld it shine,
And he knew that it was mine—

And into my garden stole
When the night had veil'd the pole;
In the morning glad I see
My foe outstretch'd beneath the tree

50

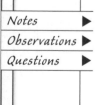

Notes ▶
Observations ▶
Questions ▶

William Blake

BEFORE READING

Why I Admire This Poem

One of the things I am smitten with about this poem is the way Blake creates the cold and calculating tone of the narrator. It's chilling. He reminds me of Montresor, the narrator in Edgar Allan Poe's "The Cask of Amontillado," who tells how he took his revenge on his friend Fortunato for a perceived insult. While Montresor tells his story in a short story several pages in length, Blake does much the same thing in a sixteen-line poem.

"A Poison Tree" is a study of anger and revenge and how anger can lead to more harm when it is encouraged to grow. Using the first-person point of view, Blake allows the narrator to lay bare his deliberate steps to entice a foe into being a victim of the narrator's cold-hearted plot. To make the poem even more chilling, the narrator utters not a hint of remorse at the sight of his *foe outstretch'd beneath the tree.*

Companion Poem

Consider this poem in conjunction with "Summertime Sharing," by Nikki Grimes. Grimes's poem is about acts of friendship and is a good contrast to Blake's poem of anger and revenge.

Special Words to Work Through

Because the poem was written at the end of the eighteenth century, it contains a few words—*wrath, foe, deceitful,* and *wiles*—that may stump some of your students. If your students would benefit from discussing these troublesome words ahead of time, write the words on the board and ask whether anyone in the class can define them. Before turning to the dictionary, you could invite students to see whether they can deduce the meaning of a challenging word from its context. The four words that I mentioned above are all within the first two stanzas of the poem, and they are used in a way that makes their meaning fairly evident.

Ask your students to underline any words that are unfamiliar to them as they read the poem. After they have read the poem a couple of times, ask them about the words that were troublesome. If some students still have difficulty with any of the words, ask for volunteers to explain the words in question. (I'm especially taken with *wrath*, which *sounds* mean and nasty.)

THEMES, ISSUES, CONCEPTS

• anger
• getting even
• resolution of anger

LITERARY TERMS

• tone
• mood
• rhyme
• quatrain
• plot
• metaphor

ORGANIZERS

• Tone
• Plot Structure

51

FIRST READING: MEETING THE POEM

We have no idea what the narrator's foe did to him to cause him to seek revenge, and there's no point trying to guess. It could have been something that he only *thought* this person did to him. Blake speaks in metaphorical terms, perhaps showing the reader what can happen if we do not address our grievances. After all, in the first two lines of the poem, when he was angry with his friend, he says, *I told my wrath, my wrath did end*. However, with his foe it's a different story.

CLOSE READING: GETTING TO KNOW THE POEM

One thing that strikes me about Blake's poem is how we can clearly see the plot unfolding. Each stanza carries the poem (and the narrator's plan for revenge) closer to its conclusion. There's no stopping it. The narrator is methodical in the execution of his plan. He watered his wrath *Night and morning with my tears*. But it is the next two lines, I find, that give the clearest insight into the narrator, when he says that he *sunned* his wrath *with my smiles/And with soft deceitful wiles*. For me, that's the turning point, the moment when we know something terrible is going to happen. And it does, as the poem ends with the narrator's foe *outstretch'd beneath the tree* that bore such deadly fruit.

Since Blake's poem is metaphorical, the foe's death is metaphorical as well. What could it mean? Have your students discuss ways in which the *foe* is metaphorically *killed* by the narrator. For example, it could mean that the *foe* is no longer a part of the person's life.

Noticing Tone and Mood

Tone in poetry is a tricky thing, because the term is often used interchangeably with *mood*. And there's no reason for your students to struggle over the subtle nuances that distinguish the two terms. *Mood* is the general atmosphere or feeling created in a poem, like the mood of desolation in "Abandoned Farmhouse," by Ted Kooser, or the mood of celebration in "Ode to Family Photographs," by Gary Soto. As readers, we recognize that mood and often react to it. We may feel happy, for example, when we read the Soto poem. On the other hand, *tone* is more the poet's attitude toward the reader—she may be arrogant or formal—or toward the subject of the poem. I think we can say that the tone of "A Poison Tree" is cold and calculating. And I think your students will hear that in the poem.

To help your students understand the concept of tone in "A Poison Tree," distribute the **Tone** organizer and ask them to respond to the questions (it may help if they have had a chance to discuss their ideas with other students in a small group):

- How does the narrator feel toward his *foe*?
- What words does the narrator use that convey his feelings?
- What tone comes through in this poem? What attitude does the narrator have toward his *foe* and to his plan?

Students might notice that in the first stanza Blake's narrator uses the word *wrath* three times and *angry* twice. The word *foe* appears three times in the poem. We also find the phrase *deceitful wiles*.

Noticing Rhyme

Nearly all the rhyming words in the poem are one-syllable words. They are strong words to place at the end the lines, most of which end with some sort of stop punctuation, a period or a semicolon. Poets tend to place important words at the ends of lines, whether or not the lines rhyme. Taking another look at the rhyming words, we see such words as *end, foe, fears, tears, wiles, night, stole*. Can your students see how these words are crucial to the poem?

Noticing Quatrain Structure

Blake's poem is written in quatrains, a four-line stanza with some sort of rhyme scheme. In this poem, the scheme is the traditional *aabb*. In other words, each quatrain contains two couplets, two rhyming lines. In addition to noting the end words, take a look at the first words in the last three stanzas: *and*. The conjunction at the start of the lines carries the plot of the poem along by introducing something new but also connects the stanza to the one that came before it. This technique, in addition to the rhyme scheme of two couplets, helps hold the poem together.

Noticing Plot

After your students have had a chance to read the poem and have cleared up any vocabulary problems, distribute the **Plot Structure** organizer. It is a series of four plot boxes, one for each stanza in the poem. Something happens in each stanza to advance the narrative. Have your students reread the poem and write down in each box, as specifically as they can, what happens in that stanza. This organizer and a brief discussion of the poem will prompt students to talk about the cause-effect relationship that so frequently fuels a plot.

Noticing Metaphor

Throughout the poem, Blake uses the metaphor (a direct comparison without *like* or *as*) of a tree to show how anger can be nurtured and bear bitter fruit. He begins his metaphor at the end of the first stanza, when his wrath *did grow*. In the second stanza, he explains what he did to encourage his wrath. The third stanza shows the

53

fruits of his anger—*an apple bright*—and that his foe knew it belonged to the narrator. The final stanza brings Blake's horror story to a close when his foe stole into the garden to taste the fruit, only to be found in the morning *outstretch'd beneath the tree*. The narrator explains his plot very calmly and deliberately.

AFTER READING: KNOWING THE POEM FOREVER

Say It Out Loud

What's a good way to present this poem to a group? A student could read it straight through by himself or herself. But *how* should it be read? What tone of voice would one use? How could one convey the calculating nature of the narrator? Although at first I thought the poem could most effectively be presented by a single reader, as I read it again and again, I changed my mind. As the plot unfolds and the tension mounts, adding a voice or two in unison readings of each stanza could be very effective. Nothing overdramatic, just a calm but more full-bodied reading showing the narrator's character.

Write About It

Have students explore one of these ideas in their writer's notebook:

1. Have you ever planned revenge or wanted to get back at someone who you felt treated you poorly? Did you carry out your plan? Did it have the effect on the other person that you anticipated? How did it affect you?

2. How do you generally deal with anger at another person, especially a friend? Will you explain to that person why you are angry? Or, would you, like Blake's narrator, allow the anger to grow until it results in worse things happening?

3. Imagine that you are the narrator of Blake's poem. Write another quatrain or two that shows how what you did to your foe affected you. Are you pleased with the "success" of your plan? Are you filled with remorse and regret for your actions? Do you hope that you have sent a message to other foes not to mess with you?

4. Here's a list of some of the key words in this poem: *end, foe, fears, tears, wiles, night, stole, angry, deceitful, wiles.* Open your writer's notebook to a blank page and write down whatever you can when you look at this list. Write phrases or sentences, or use the words as the basis for writing a poem.

Issues/Themes/Topics for Discussion

- Getting even

- Importance of expressing feelings

- Nonviolent resolution of conflict

- Dealing with anger

Book Bridges

"The Cask of Amontillado," by Edgar Allan Poe. Read this short story and look for things that Montresor says that are similar in tone and intention to what Blake's narrator in "A Poison Tree" says.

Weasel, by Cynthia DeFelice. A story of evil, guilt, and the need for revenge, set in Ohio in 1839, a time when "Indian fighters" were paid to kill Indians to make the territory safe for settlers.

For fourth and fifth graders, the books in Phyllis Reynolds Naylor's boys-girls battle series, like *The Girls Get Even*, *Boys Against Girls*, *Who Won the War?*, and *Boys in Control*. You can find out more about these books by going to www.amazon.com and searching *phyllis reynolds naylor boy girl battle*.

Related Poems

www.everypoet.com/archive/poetry/william_blake/william_blake_contents.htm has all the poems in Blake's *Songs of Innocence* and *Songs of Experience*.

Online Resources

- You can find some good biographical information on William Blake at the website of the Academy of American Poets: www.poets.org/poet.php/prmPID/116. The site always features about a dozen Blake poems.

- Your students might be interested in learning more about Blake, the engraver and painter. For examples of his visual art, go to: www.ibiblio.org/wm/paint/auth/blake/

Tone in "A Poison Tree"

How does the narrator feel toward his "foe"?

What words does he use that convey his feelings?

What tone comes through in this poem? What attitude does he have toward his "foe" and to his plan?

© 2011 by Paul B. Janeczko from *Reading Poetry in the Middle Grades*. Portsmouth, NH: Heinemann.

Name _____ Date _____ Class _____

Plot Structure in "A Poison Tree"

Stanza 1

Stanza 2

Stanza 3

Stanza 4

Summertime Sharing

Nikki Grimes

Danitra sits hunched on the stoop and pouts.
I ask her what there is to pout about.
"Nothin' much," she says to me,
but then I see her eyes following the ice cream man.

I shove my hand into my pocket
and find the change there where I left it.
"Be right back," I yell, running down the street.
Me and my fast feet are there and back in just two shakes.

Danitra breaks the Popsicle in two and gives me half.
The purple ice trickles down her chin. I start to laugh.
Her teeth flash in one humongous grin,
telling me she's glad that I'm her friend without even saying a word.

Notes ▶
Observations ▶
Questions ▶

From *Reading Poetry in the Middle Grades*. Portsmouth, NH: Heinemann. © 1997 by Nikki Grimes from *Meet Danitra Brown*, published by HarperCollins Publishers. Reprinted by permission of Writers House, Inc. Photocopies for classroom use not to exceed 100 copies per school.

> ## SUMMERTIME SHARING

Nikki Grimes

BEFORE READING

Why I Admire This Poem

When I read poems by Nikki Grimes, I expect that she will be short and sweet and speak in a way that will engage young readers. She rarely disappoints me. "Summertime Sharing" is from her wonderful book, *Meet Danitra Brown*. (Danitra returns in *Danitra Brown, Class Clown.*) Grimes does two things in this poem of friendship that I find noteworthy. First, Danitra's friend notices that she isn't herself and asks her *what there is to pout about*. Then, when she notices Danitra eyeing the ice cream man, she leaps into action, racing off to catch him. She returns *in just two shakes* with a Popsicle for her friend. This act of friendship merits a return kindness from Danitra, who splits the Popsicle in two and gives half of it to her friend. A lovely poem of true friendship, in which Danitra flashes a grin that tells her friend that *she's glad that I'm her friend without even saying a word.*

Companion Poem

Consider this simple, sweet poem in conjunction with "A Poison Tree," because the two poems raise opposite issues. Also, whereas William Blake speaks metaphorically in his poem, Grimes is concrete as she depicts one act of friendship.

Special Words to Work Through

"Summertime Sharing" is a simple poem, so there are only a couple of words that your students might need help with: *stoop* and *pouts*. The former is used as a noun rather than as a verb, which gives you the chance to discuss how words do double duty in English. Can your students think of other words that might be used as different parts of speech? Write a few of their answers on the board so the class can see them and understand their various meetings. If your students have trouble coming up with some words for the list, start them off with some examples: *race, act, play, train, visit, fold.*

Distribute copies of the **Double-Duty Words** organizer, which asks your students to list ten words that can be used as different parts of speech and to explain the meaning of each word. (This is a good exercise for students to work on in groups of two or three.)

THEMES, ISSUES, CONCEPTS

- African American poet
- friendship
- sharing

LITERARY TERMS

- structure
- word choice
- alliteration

ORGANIZERS

- Double-Duty Words

59

FIRST READING: MEETING THE POEM

Most kids in your class will have a lot to say about friendship, so it is a good subject for a class discussion after reading this poem. You can begin by asking them what makes a good friend and write their responses on the board. Can they see any similarity in the items on the board? Can they "read" their friends the way the narrator of this poem reads Danitra? Can they think of any times when their friends "read" them and helped them? It's easy to be friends with someone when things are going well, but do they have the patience to look carefully when things are out of whack as they are at the beginning of "Summertime Sharing"?

CLOSE READING: GETTING TO KNOW THE POEM

I don't know where I'd be without my friends, which is why I selected this poem. I wanted a poem about friendship but one that would show a friendship that is not always as smooth sailing as we would like our friendships to be. In "Summertime Sharing" a friendship has hit a snag, even though it is a minor issue and easily remedied. I want students to take from this poem the notion that we need to pay attention to our friends, so we can adjust and help when we sense that something is amiss. You can ask them to think of a time when a small act made all the difference to the mood they were in.

Noticing Structure

Grimes writes her poem in three quatrains, although they do not follow the traditional rhyme scheme. Hers is *aabc*—in other words, a couplet followed by two lines that do not rhyme with any other lines in the poem. You might remind your students that the quatrains in "A Poison Tree," by William Blake, each contain two couplets—that is, the rhyme scheme *aabb*. Other rhyme schemes that often appear in quatrains are *abab, abba,* and *abcb*. Since each quatrain is a stanza, they are like paragraphs in prose, telling about a single incident while moving the narrative forward.

Noticing Word Choice

Ask your students to take another look at the words they underlined when they read the poem the first time. They probably noticed some examples of Grimes' excellent word choice. Look at the first line: *hunched* and *pouts* are such expressive words, aren't they? Both provide a visual image. We can *see* someone hunched over. And we know what it looks like when we pout. With those two words, Grimes shows us right off that Danitra is not in a very good place. Then, she not only rhymes *pouts* and *about* but also uses both words at the end of the second line, when the narrator asks Danitra *what there is to pout about.* Danitra's short reply—*Nothin' much*— is another indication that something is bothering the narrator's friend.

My favorite line in the poem is, *The purple ice trickles down her chin. I start to laugh.* Isn't *trickle* the perfect word to describe what the purple ice does? Doesn't the word slow the "story" down a bit, too? Can't you just see it? And *feel* it? And can't you hear the laughter? It's word choices like these that make this poem so alive.

Noticing Alliteration

Did anyone in your class catch the neat expression in the last line of the second stanza, *Me and my fast feet are there and back in just two shakes*? Grimes also uses alliteration here, repeating the initial consonant sound in *fast feet.* Alliteration often happens by accident when we are writing a poem. It may be something we wouldn't even notice if we didn't read the poem aloud. That's why I believe reading aloud is a crucial part of writing and reading poetry. When you assign poems, implore your students to read them out loud. They don't have to make it a big production. Just sitting on their bed alone and reading the poem aloud a time or two is enough for them to *hear* the poem.

AFTER READING: **KNOWING THE POEM FOREVER**

Say It Out Loud

This poem offers some nice presentation possibilities. It could be read by one person as the narrator, with a second reader taking Danitra's *Nothin' much.* There are also actions in the poem that can be incorporated into an oral presentation:

- "Danitra sits hunched on the stoop and pouts."
- "I see her eyes following the ice cream man."
- "I shove my hand into my pocket"
- "I yell, running down the street."
- "Danitra breaks the Popsicle in two and gives me half."

With some care and imagination, "Summertime Sharing" can be presented as a short scene in the lives of these good friends.

Write About It

This poem prompts students to think about the nature of friendship. Here are a few ideas they might explore in their writer's notebook:

1. Make a list of people you consider to be your closest friends. How do you *show* these people that you value their friendship? Name some things that they have done to *show* you their friendship. Think hard about these questions. Don't let yourself off the hook by saying, "Oh, we don't have to *do* anything. We *know* we're best friends." *How* do you know you're best friends?

2. Write an email to one of the people on your list, explaining how much his or her friendship means to you. You don't have to send it if you don't want to, but it would be nice if you did.

3. Write a short personal narrative about an experience you had with one of your friends, a time when your friend showed her/his friendship or you showed yours. You can also write about a time when your friend disappointed you and how you reacted to that experience. Or you can write about a time you disappointed a friend.

4. Write text message to a friend using the common texting abbreviations.

Issues/Themes/Topics for Discussion

- Friendship
- Sharing

Related Poems

Nikki Grimes has an impressive list of poetry books, but three you should move to the top of your to-read list are: *Stepping Out With Grandma Mac, A Pocketful of Poems,* and *Hopscotch Love.*

I included "Summertime Sharing" in my anthology *Very Best (Almost) Friends,* along with other good poems of friendship like:

"Peter the Pain," by Kalli Dakos

"I Still Have Everything You Gave Me," by Naomi Shihab Nye

"Lonesome," by Myra Cohn Livingston

"The Marmalade Man Makes a Dance to Mend Us," by Nancy Willard

Also take a look at *I Like You, If You Like Me: Poems of Friendship,* an anthology edited by Myra Cohn Livingston, that includes the work of poets Richard Wilbur, Gwendolyn Brooks, Robert Frost, and Carl Sandburg.

Book Bridges

Novels about friendship abound, but here are a few especially good ones:

Freak the Mighty, by Rodman Philbrick. Two social outcasts become firm friends in this novel that inspired the feature film *The Mighty.*

Millicent Min, Girl Genius, by Lisa Yee. Millicent may have a high IQ, but she still has a lot to learn about friendship.

The Misfits, by James Howe. Four friends resolve to stand up to their classmates' bullying.

P.S. Longer Letter Later and *Snail Mail No More,* by Paula Danziger and Ann M. Martin. Two friends send school stories across the miles.

Rosie and Michael by Judith Viorst. This simple story is a wonderful two-voice opportunity for kids.

Online Resources

• Nikki Grimes puts a lot of work into her website, www.nikkigrimes.com. Of course, she has detailed information about all of her books, but she includes so much more about her life and the issues that mean so much to her. She offers solid tips for young people on writing, as well as tips for teachers. When you visit Nikki Grimes's website, you are in the poetry zone!

Double-Duty Words in "Summertime Sharing" _____

Word: **Meanings:**	**Word** **Meanings:**
Word: **Meanings:**	**Word** **Meanings:**
Word: **Meanings:**	**Word** **Meanings:**
Word: **Meanings:**	**Word** **Meanings:**
Word: **Meanings:**	**Word** **Meanings:**

The Wreck of the Hesperus

Henry Wadsworth Longfellow

It was the schooner *Hesperus*,
That sailed the wint'ry sea;
And the skipper had taken his little daughter,
To bear him company.

Blue were her eyes as the fairy-flax,
Her cheeks like the dawn of day,
And her bosom white as the hawthorn buds
That ope in the month of May.

The skipper he stood beside the helm,
His pipe was in his mouth,
And he watched how the veering flaw did blow
The smoke now West, now South.

Then up and spake an old sailor,
Had sailed the Spanish Main,
"I pray thee put into yonder port,
For I fear a hurricane.

"Last night, the moon had a golden ring,
And tonight no moon we see!"
The skipper, he blew a whiff from his pipe,
And a scornful laugh laughed he.

Colder and louder blew the wind,
A gale from the Northeast;
The snow fell hissing in the brine,
And the billows frothed like yeast.

Down came the storm, and smote amain
The vessel in its strength;
She shuddered and paused, like a frighted steed,
Then leaped her cable's length.

"Come hither! come hither! my little daughter,
And do not tremble so;
For I can weather the roughest gale
That ever wind did blow."

He wrapped her warm in his seaman's coat
Against the stinging blast;
He cut a rope from a broken spar,
And bound her to the mast.

"O father! I hear the church bells ring,
O say what may it be?"
"'Tis a fog-bell on a rock-bound coast!"
And he steered for the open sea.

"O father! I hear the sound of guns,
O say what may it be?"
"Some ship in distress, that cannot live
In such an angry sea!"

"O father! I see a gleaming light,
O say what may it be?"
But the father answered never a word,
A frozen corpse was he.

Lashed to the helm, all stiff and stark,
With his face turned to the skies,
The lantern gleamed through the gleaming snow
On his fixed and glassy eyes.

Then the maiden clasped her hands and prayed
That saved she might be;
And she thought of Christ who stilled the wave
On the Lake of Galilee.

And fast through the midnight dark and drear,
Through the whistling sleet and snow,
Like a sheeted ghost, the vessel swept
Towards the reef of Norman's Woe.

From *Reading Poetry in the Middle Grades*. Portsmouth, NH: Heinemann. © by Henry Wadsworth Longfellow from *Ballads and Other Poems*.

And ever the fitful gusts between
A sound came from the land;
It was the sound of the trampling surf,
On the rocks and the hard sea-sand.

The breakers were right beneath her bows,
She drifted a dreary wreck,
And a whooping billow swept the crew
Like icicles from her deck.

She struck where the white and fleecy waves
Looked soft as carded wool,
But the cruel rocks, they gored her sides
Like the horns of an angry bull.

Her rattling shrouds, all sheathed in ice,
With the masts went by the board;
Like a vessel of glass she stove and sank,
Ho! ho! the breakers roared!

At daybreak, on the bleak sea-beach,
A fisherman stood aghast,
To see the form of a maiden fair
Lashed close to a drifting mast.

The salt sea was frozen on her breast,
The salt tears in her eyes;
And he saw her hair, like the brown seaweed,
On the billows fall and rise.

Such was the wreck of the *Hesperus*,
In the midnight and the snow!
Christ save us all from a death like this
On the reef of Norman's Woe!

Henry Wadsworth Longfellow

BEFORE READING

Why I Admire This Poem

Many readers in an age of instant messaging and YouTube may find it hard to believe that Henry Wadsworth Longfellow was a poet with a rock-star following in his own country as well as in Europe during the mid-1800s. However, I'm not surprised at his popularity. Longfellow can spin a good story in verse, often filled with excitement, daring, and danger. And let's not forget that some of his more famous longer poems, like "Evangeline" and "Hiawatha," are enduring love stories. Longfellow wrote at a time when it was common to spend an evening listening to someone—often the poet himself—read poems aloud in a finely appointed parlor. Such evenings weren't exactly poetry slams, but it was a favored form of entertainment and edification for the educated populations in places like Boston and New York. Longfellow's contemporaries in the United States included William Cullen Bryant and John Greenleaf Whittier. In England, he gave Alfred Lord Tennyson a run for his money on the lecture circuit.

"The Wreck of the *Hesperus*" is a wonderful example of a so-called parlor poem that begs to be read aloud, perhaps with a bit of gusto and exaggeration. It is clearly a poem to have fun with. But more about that later.

Special Words to Work Through

Although the narrative of "The Wreck of the *Hesperus*" is straightforward, some historical notes might help students place the poem in its correct nautical context.

- Norman's Woe is a rock and reef formation not far from the outer harbor of Gloucester, Massachusetts, north of Boston. Longfellow based his poem on a tragic wreck on Norman's Woe in the winter of 1839, when the schooner *Favorite*, sailing from Wiscasset, Maine, crashed on the rocks. Twenty bodies washed ashore, including a woman tied to a piece of the ship. He took the name of the ship in his poem from the *Hesperus*, a ship that wrecked near Boston.

- The Spanish Main was the mainland cost of the Spanish Empire, which included Florida, Mexico, and Central America, as well as the northern coast of South America. The term came to refer to the seas around the Spanish colonies in the Caribbean.

- A schooner is a sailing vessel with at least two masts, with the foremast usually shorter than other masts.

THEMES, ISSUES, CONCEPTS

- classic poem
- sailing
- shipwrecks

LITERARY TERMS

- form: ballad
- plot
- metaphor
- simile

ORGANIZERS

- Episode Blocks

69

Because this poem was written over 150 years ago, the language may present a problem for some students. Among the terms that might need explanation are:

- *fairy-flax*: a perennial plant in the herb genus that has blue flowers; see www.paghat.com/flax-blue.html
- *veering flaw*: changing wind
- *spake*: spoke
- *gale*: strong wind
- *spar*: a stout pole used in masts
- *carded wool*: soft wool after tangles and knots have been removed
- *gored*: pierced, as by a horn of a bull
- *mast*: tallest upright part of a sailing ship that holds the sails

FIRST READING: MEETING THE POEM

Your students may find this poem quaint or corny, even melodramatic, and by the standards of twenty-first-century American culture it might very well be all of the above. However, if you can get your students to look beyond their prejudices, they will see a poem of high drama, a filmmaker's dream, with its rampaging storm, a doomed ship, and a helpless child. No wonder it was a huge hit in parlor readings.

You might also give your students a chance to explore the poem as an example of character development. You can divide your class into four groups and have each look at a character in the poem: the captain, his daughter, the old sailor, and the narrator. Ask each group to look for evidence in the poem that helps explain or describe each character. They should look for physical details as well as details that illustrate the personality of each character. This exploration will help the students when they make an oral presentation of the poem.

Even though we know from the title that there is a shipwreck in the poem, the fun of the poem is in the telling. Ask your students how the following details in the first few stanzas might play out in a film:

- "Blue were her eyes as the fairy-flax."
- "The skipper he stood beside the helm,/His pipe was in his mouth."
- "The skipper, he blew a whiff from his pipe,/And a scornful laugh laughed he."
- "Colder and louder blew the wind,/A gale from the Northeast."
- Wave "billows frothed like yeast."

Can your students see the visual images that Longfellow used? Can they hear the wind? The same details that could make this a dramatic film make it a dramatic poem. You might want to look at some of the dramatic scenes late in the movie,

Titanic, to give your students some examples. Ask your students to look for other images in the poem that might translate well to film.

CLOSE READING: GETTING TO KNOW THE POEM

Noticing Form

Although the ballad form does not have the consistency found in other poetic forms—the sonnet, the limerick, and the villanelle, for example—you can expect a ballad to have some of these characteristics:

- A narrative. Often a ballad tells a simple story, one that depicts dramatic events that are likely to be tragic and strange. Many ballads tell of flawed and fatal relationships between lovers, between family members, or between people and the supernatural.

- Simple language, which reflects the genre's roots as a poetic form used by people without a great deal of formal training in language or poetry.

- Four-line stanzas, usually with an *abcb* rhyme scheme, sometimes *abab*. In both cases, the second and fourth lines rhyme—a constant in most ballads.

- A rhythm pattern in which the first and third lines have four stressed (or accented) syllables, while the rhyming lines—the second and the fourth— have just three stressed syllables.

- Repetition, which is often expressed in a refrain, a group of lines repeated as a transition to another section of the narrative. Some ballads have an incremental refrain that differs slightly as the poem progresses.

- Dialogue between characters.

- Usually told in the third person. Sometimes a first-person narrator tells the story and appears as a character. How would this poem be different if it were told from a different point of view? Ask your students to "rewrite" part of the poem—stanzas 2–15, for example—in the first-person point of view. Does this revision have a different feel? Does it work better than the original? What is gained and lost with such a change in point of view?

Noticing Plot

Because "The Wreck of the *Hesperus*" is a narrative, having students complete the **Episode Blocks** organizer as they read the poem might help them see the narrative arc Longfellow follows in the poem. An alternative is to have the students complete a narrative plot line that shows a plot's rising and falling action (see Figure 4). Use self-adhesive notes to stick to the plot line so you change the episodes if you need to.

71

Figure 4

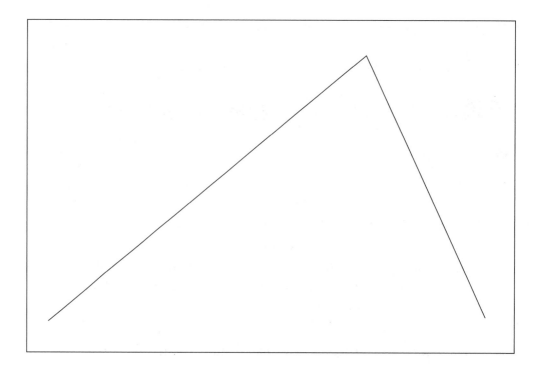

As the students work, ask them to look for warnings or foreshadowing of what will happen later.

One of the characteristics of a ballad is dialogue, although there isn't much in this poem. However, make sure that the students recognize that stanzas 10, 11, and 12 all begin with the daughter speaking two lines, followed, in stanzas 10 and 11, by the father's reassurances. He does not reply after that because, as we learn in stanza 12, *A frozen corpse was he.*

Noticing Figurative Language

Longfellow's poems are filled with rich, figurative language, and "The Wreck of the *Hesperus*" is no exception. His skill at using metaphors and similes is especially evident in stanzas 15–20. No doubt your students will notice similes such as these:

- *And a whooping billow swept the crew/Like icicles from her deck* (stanza 17).

- *. . . the white and fleecy waves/Looked soft as carded wool* (stanza 18).

- *Her rattling shrouds, all sheathed in ice . . . /Like a vessel of glass* (stanza 19).

There are of course many other places in the poem where Longfellow uses figurative language. Divide your class into four small groups. Assign each group to read five or six stanzas of the poem, underlining examples of metaphors and similes they notice. Ask each group to report their findings to the class.

Noticing Details

Longfellow also uses vivid details to make his story come alive. Ask your students to note examples of details they find in the poem. They may notice details such as these:

- *The snow fell hissing in the brine* (sound) (stanza 6).

- *The lantern gleamed through the gleaming snow/On his fixed and glassy eyes* (sight) (stanza 13).

- *The salt sea was frozen on her breast,/The salt tears in her eyes* (touch) (stanza 21) .

AFTER READING: **KNOWING THE POEM FOREVER**

Say It Out Loud

An obvious way to perform this poem is to assign parts: the skipper, his daughter, the old sailor, and, of course, the narrator, who has the largest part. The narrator, however, need not be an individual reader. In fact, having the narration read by a small chorus could give the performance a dramatic wallop.

A careful reading of the poem will suggest other ways to perform it. Perhaps the first 14 stanzas can be read by individuals rather than by a chorus. For example, a girl could read stanza 2, which describes the daughter, as well as stanzas 13 and 14, when the girl is *lashed to the helm, all stiff and stark*. Stanzas 15–20, in which the storm is most ferocious, could be read by a chorus that captures the intensity of the storm. Perhaps a couple of your students would like to try creating a dramatic reading of the exchange between the daughter and the father.

Issues/Themes/Topics for Discussion

- Sailing
- Sea disasters
- Shipwrecks, particularly the *Titanic*
- Sunken treasure
- Underwater archeology

Related Poems

"The Wreck of Rivermouth" by John Greenleaf Whittier and "The Wreck of the Edmund Fitzgerald" by Gordon Lightfoot, both widely available on the Internet.

73

Other poems by Longfellow:

Henry Wadsworth Longfellow, edited by Frances Schoonmaker, a volume in the Sterling Poetry for Young People series, contains a sampling of Longfellow's poems as well as information about his life.

The Penguin Classics edition of Longfellow's *Selected Poems* contains a good selection, including two of his longer poems, "Evangeline" and "The Courtship of Miles Standish," as well as a few other poems that might interest your students: "Paul Revere's Ride," "The Skeleton in Armor," and "The Village Blacksmith." Many of his poems can be used in other content areas, especially social studies.

A number of websites include the ballads and narrative poetry of Robert W. Service, including two favorites: "The Cremation of Sam McGee" and "The Shooting of Dan McGraw." Try these links:

www.robertwservice.com/ www.internal.org/list_poems.phtml?authorID=10
www.poemhunter.com/robert-w-service

Book Bridges

Fiction:

Kensuke's Kingdom, by Michael Morpurgo. An exciting novel about a storm at sea and life on a deserted island. Or so Michael thinks, until he discovers otherwise.

Shipwreck, by Gordon Korman. Six troubled kids are sent on a monthlong journey on the Pacific Ocean in a small boat. The title of this exciting novel tells what awaits them.

The Silent Storm, by Sherry Garland. Alyssa, the thirteen-year-old protagonist, hasn't spoken since her parents died in a hurricane. Now another storm is bearing down on Galveston, where she lives with her grandmother.

Sand Dollar Summer, by Kimberly Jones. The twelve-year-old protagonist must deal with her uncontrollable fear of the ocean, while her mother recovers from an auto accident in Maine.

Nonfiction:

Shipwreck, by Richard Platt. A DK Eyewitness book with lavish illustrations and photographs and lots of information about famous wrecks and underwater archeology.

Hurricanes, by Seymour Simon. This book contains all that young readers would want to know about where hurricanes come from and why they can be so destructive.

Online Resources

Famous shipwrecks links:

- www.shipwreckexpo.com/famousshipwrecks.htm
- www.wreckhunter.net/famouswrecks.htm
- www.yourdiscovery.com/best_of/wreck_detectives/shipwrecks/index.shtml

Music:

- *Rogue's Gallery: Pirate Ballads, Sea Songs, and Chanteys* (http://
  en.wikipedia.org/wiki/Rogue%27s_Gallery:_Pirate_Ballads,_Sea_Songs,_
  and_Chanteys) is a compilation album of sea shanties performed by a
  wide array of artists, ranging from Sting to Bryan Ferry, representing a
  variety of genres.

Books:

- *Sea Songs and Ballads,* by Christopher Stone, a downloadable book available at: books.google.com

Episode Blocks in "The Wreck of the *Hesperus*" _____

Read through "The Wreck of the *Hesperus*" to understand the story that
Longfellow tells. Then read the poem a second time, paying special attention to the episodes he uses to tell his story. In each of the blocks below,
write one episode that is important to the story. Mark off where the story
reaches its climax before the falling action and the end of the poem.

Every Cat Has a Story

Naomi Shihab Nye

The yellow one from the bakery
smelled like a cream puff—
she followed us home.
We buried our faces
in her sweet fur.

One cat hid her head
while I practiced violin.
But she came out for piano.
At night she played sonatas
on my quilt.

One cat built a secret nest
in my socks.

One sat in the window
staring up the street all day
while we were at school.

One cat loved
the radio dial.

One cat almost
smiled.

Notes ▶
Observations ▶
Questions ▶

▶ **EVERY CAT HAS A STORY**

Naomi Shihab Nye

BEFORE READING

Why I Admire This Poem

When Naomi Shihab Nye publishes a new book of poems, I can't wait to get my hands on it. I always try to include one of her poems in my anthologies, and I had the good fortune to work with her on our joint anthology, *I Feel a Little Jumpy Around You: Paired Poems by Men and Women* (www.paulbjaneczko.com). "Every Cat Has a Story" is an example of how this woman works her craft. It delights the reader—even those who are not "cat people"—and offers students and teachers a lesson on how details can become poetic. She teaches us as readers and writers how to pay attention to the ordinary and see the remarkable.

The poem stands as an example of what a successful list poem can be. Any good list poem is more than just a list, of course. It needs to have the details, language, and economy that we expect in a poem. Nye covers all these bases. Look at her economical use of language, how she makes decisions throughout the poem, first deciding what to say about each of the cats, then deciding on the best words to portray the nature of each cat through details and actions.

Look as well at the sense details in the opening stanza:

- *yellow one*—sight

- *smelled like a cream puff*—smell

- *buried our faces/in her sweet fur*—touch/smell

Also, note the action—*she followed us home*—and the nonaction—letting the family bury their faces in *her sweet fur*. Nye demonstrates the same care throughout the poem.

Companion Poems

Nye's poem goes well with "Seeing the World," by Steven Herrick, because both poems are about really looking at the world. The narrator in Herrick's poems experiences the thrill of seeing the world from high on a rooftop. Nye, on the other hand, sees the cats in her life in close-up. I list a few other cat poems in the Related Poems section.

Special Words to Work Through

One of the beauties of this poem is its simple language—no big words that could trip up most students. However, your students may not know that a *sonata* is a musical composition for one or more solo instruments. (You might play Beethoven's

THEMES, ISSUES, CONCEPTS

- surprise in poetry
- pets
- testing products on animals

LITERARY TERMS

- list poem
- images
- sense details
- structure
- personification
- line break

ORGANIZERS

- Sense Details
- My Pets

"Moonlight Sonata"; see the Online Resources section for two sources.) Sonatas are frequently written for violin and piano. Announcing that the *cat played sonatas/on my quilt*, Nye is referring to the actions of a cat when it stretches its front legs out and moves its paws back and forth, reminiscent of someone playing the piano. I'm sure that the cat lovers in the class will be happy to demonstrate this feline action.

FIRST READING: MEETING THE POEM

Preparing to read "Every Cat Has a Story" is a good time to revisit a question I posed earlier in this book: what do your students look for in a good poem, either one they read or one they write? As a result of that discussion, you might have a preliminary list of the qualities your students expect in a poem posted in your classroom. Ask your students if Nye's poem suggests other qualities to add to the list. Can they find examples in the poem of the qualities already listed? Do they want to modify anything on the list?

One thing I look for in a poem is surprise. Not the surprise of a shocking ending, but more subtle surprises. I love to be surprised by how a poet uses language. Spots in a poem that make me say "Wow." Nye's poem certainly has wow moments for me, but I also love the ending of the poem. I didn't *almost* smile at her last stanza. I *did* smile—a delightful surprise. Is the poet saying that the cat is "almost" human?

CLOSE READING: GETTING TO KNOW THE POEM

Noticing Images

At the heart of a good poem are images that appeal to the senses. It is through these images that we can see and feel and hear what the poet is saying. Distribute the **Sense Details** organizer and ask your students to fill it out after they've read the poem with an eye attentive to sense details. Not every poem appeals to all the senses, but a good poet is tuned in to them.

Nye uses sight, smell, and touch images in her poem. (And taste, if you consider that cream puff!) But notice how none of the sense details seem forced, as if she *needed* to include more senses. They feel perfectly at home in the poem.

Noticing Structure

Each stanza in this poem is like a paragraph in a prose story. In each one Nye talks about one cat. The stanzas vary in length, but my favorite is the last stanza with only four words in it. I love how she breaks the four words into two lines, with *almost* at the end of the first line in the stanza and *smiled* all by itself in the final line of the poem. Nye puts the important words at the end of both lines, but it is the separation with the slight pause between these two words that makes the stanza so effective.

Noticing Line Breaks

This poem is a valuable lesson in line breaks. I already discussed the importance of the line break in the final stanza, but Nye does an equally effective job throughout the poem. Take a look at the end words in the first and second stanzas:

- Stanza 1: *bakery, (cream) puff, home, faces, fur*
- Stanza 2: *head, violin, piano, sonata, quilt*

These ten words carry importance for the poet. That's why she put them at the ends of lines. Ask your students to list the end word of each line in each remaining stanza. You will find that they too are important words in the poem.

Beyond that, however, take a look at all the words in the first stanza. The words on each line feel at home with each other. They belong together. Each line holds, in a sense, a complete thought.

As a line break exercise, do with this poem what I do with my poem, "Stories," on page 29. Ask your students to decide on the best line breaks. Be sure to read the prose version of the poem aloud so the class can hear what words go together. As students offer suggestions, mark them on the transparency. Insist that your students have a logical or linguistic reason for their choices. Although you may disagree with their choices, the important thing is that they have given some thought to the process. When they have exhausted the possibilities, show them the real poem (page 30). Chances are their line breaks will be close to those Nye uses in her poem.

Noticing Personification

I've talked about how the cat *played sonatas* in the second stanza. We know the cat didn't actually play sonatas, but Nye gives the cat human qualities so that the reader can visualize the cat's actions. Giving human qualities to an inanimate object is called *personification*, a device used frequently by poets.

It's easy to overuse personification and give inappropriate and silly qualities to inanimate objects. (Such over-the-top use of personification is called the *pathetic fallacy*.) For example, here are a couple of lines from Shelley: "The stars will awaken / Though the moon sleep a full hour later." And consider this line from *Jane Eyre*—not poetry, I know, but the principle still holds—"Nature must be gladsome when I was so happy."

AFTER READING: KNOWING THE POEM FOREVER

Say It Out Loud

Have a different student read each stanza. Or have one reader read each introductory noun phrase (noun, in the case of stanza 4), then have a different student read the rest of each stanza. A group of teachers I worked with staged this poem by casting the narrator of the poem as an old woman sitting in a rocking chair, stroking the cat in her lap as she reminisced about her other cats.

Write About It

Have students explore one of these ideas in their writer's notebook:

1. The narrator of the poem notices small details about how the cats behave. Try doing the same thing with your pet. Spend some time paying attention to how your pet acts. List in your writer's notebook some of those details. (Use the **My Pets** organizer to help you.) Do your details appeal to the senses? Try shaping those details into a poem of details like "Every Cat Has a Story."

2. Try writing a list poem titled "The History of My Pets." Follow the same plan for gathering information suggested above. Begin with a list of your pets and write down some sense details for each one. Remember that you want to *show* the pets to your reader, so don't settle for "details" like "my first dog was small and really cute," "that cat did the weirdest things," or "nobody would believe the things our parrot said." Those don't help us see or feel or hear your pet. Don't rush. As you think of telling details, write them down. You'll gradually build good detailed lists that you can use in your poem. [Give students who choose this option a copy of "A History of Pets," by David Huddle to use as a model. They can also use the **My Pets** organizer to capture their ideas.]

Issues/Themes/Topics for Discussion

- Michael Vick and his dog-fighting operations
- Responsible pet ownership
- Testing cosmetics on animals
- Animal experiments for medical purposes

Related Poems

"A History of Pets," by David Huddle

"The Flying Cat," by Naomi Shihab Nye

"The Two Cats," by Elizabeth Coatsworth

"The Cat Who Aspired to Higher Things," by X. J. Kennedy

Cats Are Cats, edited by Nancy Larrick

Book Bridges

Meow: Cat Stories from Around the World, by Jane Yolen. A wonderful collection of stories, sayings, and nursery rhymes from countries far and wide, enhanced by paintings of more than fifty different cats.

The Story of a Seagull and the Cat Who Taught Her to Fly, by Luis Sepulveda, translated by Margaret Sayers Peden. A dying seagull entrusts her egg to Zorba the cat. But will the cat keep its word?

Hate That Cat, by Sharon Creech. A follow-up book to her *Love That Dog.*

Spy Cat, Danger Next Door, Trapped, all by Peg Kehret. Lots of cats and adventure in the Pete the Cat series.

Toes, by Tor Seidler. After getting lost on Halloween night, the seven-toed cat of the title finds a new life with a struggling musician.

The Cat's Purr by Ashley Bryan. A wonderful tale that explains how the cat got its purr, and why cats and rats dislike each other.

Cats: How to Choose and Care for a Cat, by Laura S. Jeffrey.

Everything Cat: What Kids Really Want to Know About Cats, by Marty Crisp.

Online Resources

- Beethoven's "Moonlight Sonata." Wilhelm Kempff plays the classical piano piece at http://video.google.com/videoplay?docid=-843261094544506874#. Marcus Miller plays a jazzy version of the piece at www.dailymotion.com/video/x21por_marcus-miller-moonlight-sonata_music.

Name _____ Date _____ Class _____

Sense Details in "Every Cat Has a Story"

	Details	Senses
Stanza 1		
Stanza 2		
Stanza 3		
Stanza 4		
Stanza 5		
Stanza 6		

Name _____ Date _____ Class _____

My Pets

Pet's Name	Pet's Name	Pet's Name
Details and Senses	**Details and Senses**	**Details and Senses**

Street Painting

Ann Turner

Notes ▶
Observations ▶
Questions ▶

I watched him a long time
and this is how he did it:
Stand in front of the wall
like it's a bad dream.
Make faces.
Jam your hat down.
Pull it off.
Pop your fingers—walk
around the block and come back,
start up like you surprised
the wall's still there.

Then sigh.
Take out your paints.
Doodle around with them,
stirring and humming.
Dip a brush in,
stare at it,
take a rush forward
and dab-dab-dab
at the wall.
Soon's you know,
you got faces
and bodies and trees
like they were locked up
in that old brush
and all you had to do
was stare at it
to get a picture.

86

Ann Turner

■ **BEFORE** READING

Why I Admire This Poem

At first glance, this is a poem about creativity and the creative process. The narrator observes a street painter, then describes what he did. The poem and the painter move from chaos and frustration to calm and creation. To get a sense of what your students think of when they hear words like *creative* and *creativity*, give them the **Who Is Creative?** organizer and ask them to think about the questions presented there. Then give your students some time to fill in the chart with their views on creativity. Afterward, when they discuss their thoughts, are there common qualities in what they suggest? Write them on chart paper so it is visible as the class continues to work with the poem.

There is more going on in "Street Painting" than someone watching another person create art. It is also about letting go and taking a chance on something that is so strong you can't ignore it. Students should also note how the narrator of the poem has observed the behavior of the street painter and has learned from her observation. Will the narrator also be able to let go and follow her creative urges? The street painter needs to leave the blank wall *like it's a bad dream* and *walk/around the block and come back*, only to find out that his challenge—the blank wall—is still there. The poem is about letting things happen. Not everything will happen the way we plan it. Sometimes, the more we struggle with something, the more it resists. The street painter is stymied by the wall, but when he lets go, he can *doodle around* his paints, and *dab-dab-dab* with them until he can see *faces/and bodies and trees/like they were locked up/in that old brush.*

Companion Poem

This poem and "Seeing the World," by Steven Herrick, have an underlying theme of looking at things in a different way to see what's really there. Do your students know people who generally look at life in an unusual way? Do they know people who see things that others miss?

Special Concepts to Work Through

This poem may speak to your students more effectively if you show them some examples of street painting or graffiti. The four websites listed in the Online Resources section at the end of this unit contain enough wild examples of this urban art to

THEMES, ISSUES, CONCEPTS

- creativity
- graffiti: art or vandalism?
- risk taking

LITERARY TERMS

- images
- alliteration
- assonance
- line break

ORGANIZERS

- Who Is Creative?

87

keep you looking for hours. The nonfiction books listed under Book Bridges also contain ample and varied examples of street art.

▎FIRST▎READING: MEETING THE POEM

Before your students read "Street Painting," ask if they would consider themselves risk takers. Can they think of a time when they took a risk? What was the outcome? Can they describe a time when they considered taking a risk but decided against it? What stopped them? Was it something that a friend told them? Certainly there are situations—where physical harm is involved—when risk taking is foolish and downright dangerous. But what about when it comes to doing something creative or athletic? Is there something they've always wanted to do—like play a musical instrument or try out for a team or a club—that they have shied away from? Why? See if you can get a productive discussion going between the risk takers and your more timid students.

▎CLOSE▎READING: GETTING TO KNOW THE POEM

This is an active poem. After the opening two lines, in which the narrator watches the street painter for *a long time/and this is how he did it*, there is a lot happening. Even the title is active, as opposed to, say, "Street Painter." We get a sense of the painter's frustration in the first stanza, the way he makes faces and jams his hat down on his head, only to *pull it off*. He finally walks around the block to clear his head or perhaps to get an idea of what he will make of the wall, only to return to find *the wall's still there*.

The space between the first and second stanza is the poem's turning point. While the first stanza is active, the painter isn't working on his painting. The poet saves that for the second stanza. That's when the young painter gets down to business. Starting slowly—*sigh. Take out your paints.* After that? *Doodle ... stirring and humming ... Dip a brush ... rush forward/and dab-dab-dab/at the wall.* The painter has broken free of that constricting frustration and is making art.

Noticing Images

As you would expect in a poem about an artist painting, this is a very visual poem. The images that Turner creates help us see the action of the poem. First, the narrator *watched him for a long time*. Visual details follow. We can imagine the expression on the artist's face as he stands *in front of the wall/like it's a bad dream*. Then, see what he does after that:

Make faces.
Jam your hat down.

Pull it off.
Pop your fingers—walk
around the block

These are actions, and we see him perform them.

In the second stanza, the visual images continue as we see the artist finally beginning to work on the wall:

Take out your paints.
Doodle around with them
stirring and humming.
Dip a brush in,
stare at it,
take a rush forward
and dab-dab-dab
at that wall.

In the remainder of the poem, the painting on the wall begins to emerge. Once again we *see* those images.

Speaking of "seeing," doesn't the narrator of the poem *see* the painter and note how she approaches his art? Take a second look at the poem from the standpoint of the narrator. What is she learning about the character and personality of the painter? Have your students discuss that aspect of the poem.

Noticing Alliteration and Assonance

Even though this is a poem about seeing, it's a poem filled with lively language, a treat to the ear. Turner uses *alliteration*—repetition of initial consonant sounds—in the first stanza with the *p* sound: *Pull it off./Pop your fingers*. She also uses *assonance*—repetition of internal vowel sounds—in these lines: *Pop your fingers— walk/around the block*. Can you hear the /ah/ sound in the middle of *pop* and *block*? And there is the repetition of the /k/ sound in *around the block and come back*.

Turner uses alliteration again in the second stanza, with *doodle, dip*, and *dab-dab-dab*. These sorts of poetic devices are apt to be lost on your students if they do not read the poem aloud. It seems akin to reading a great jazz song from a piece of sheet music rather than listening to Miles Davis play it.

Noticing Line Breaks

Your students might notice that there are a lot of short lines in the poem that end with punctuation. In the first stanza, you have:

Make faces.
Jam your hat down.
Pull it off.
Pop your fingers—

Fingers isn't the end of the line, but it is followed by punctuation. The middle of the second stanza has something similar. The first six lines end with punctuation. Lines 7 and 8 are short, and line 9 ends with a period.

What is the effect of all these short lines? Read the poem aloud, and you'll hear that the short lines with end punctuation make the poem sound frenetic. There is a lot happening in the first twenty lines of the poem, and it's happening quickly. And even though the last eight lines of the poem are also short lines, only one ends with punctuation. If you read those final lines of the poem, the action feels slowed down and flows more smoothly.

AFTER READING: KNOWING THE POEM FOREVER

Say It Out Loud

Although "Street Painting" is told from the point of view of a narrator, it can be presented as an ensemble piece. The short lines in the poem, many ending with punctuation, are a perfect opportunity to have a number of students each read a single line. Also, since the first twenty lines of the poem move along at a brisk pace, it's imperative that each student read her or his line without hesitation. But don't line up the readers and move from one reader to the next—this is too tame and predictable. The reading will be a more successful performance if the readers are bunched up in a group and each line pops out without a visual cue. The final eight lines of the poem are more relaxed, so you might want to have a small chorus read that section.

Write About It

Have students explore one of these ideas in their writer's notebook:

1. Make a list of five words that describe how you feel when you are undecided about whether you should take a chance on something. Then make a list of five words that describe how you feel when you take a chance and you get the results you hoped for.

2. Write about something you do that is creative. It could be writing a poem or taking good photographs. But it can also be making up excuses for not doing your chores or homework or finding ways to have fun with your friends. We are creative in many different ways.

3. The writer's notebook is not just for words. You can draw, doodle, and mess with colored pencil, markers, and crayons in it. Even if you think you're "not good" at drawing, that shouldn't stop you from trying it in the safety of your private notebook. And, if you do draw a picture, you might want to write about the process that carried you to the drawing.

Issues/Themes/Topics for Discussion

- Taking chances
- Creativity
- Graffiti: art or vandalism?

Related Poems

"Write About a Radish," by Karla Kuskin

"Valentine for Ernest Mann," by Naomi Shihab Nye

"Poets Go Wishing," by Lilian Moore

Book Bridges

Fiction:

Bird, by Zetta Elliott. A young African American expresses himself by drawing as he struggles to make sense of his older brother's drug addiction and death.

Tagged, by Mara Purnhagen. When her high school building is hit by graffiti artists, Katie wants to find out who did that to her school, but she has feelings about the artistic merits of the graffiti and her growing affection for a coworker.

Nonfiction:

Murals: Walls That Sing, by George Ancona. A photo essay featuring forty murals on themes of social justice, cultural diversity, and community.

Painters of the Caves, by Patricia Lauber. An exploration of the the Chauvet caves of France, with walls bearing Stone Age painting.

Poetry:

Life Doesn't Frighten Me, by Maya Angelou. A poem illustrated by graffiti artist, Jean-Michel Basquiat.

Online Resources

Here are a couple of websites to visit to see some amazing street painting:

- www.weburbanist.com/2008/12/14/3d-graffiti-street-art/
- www.streetpaintingsociety.com/home/

If you want to see some incredible examples of graffiti, check out these sites:

- www.graffiti.org/
- www.graffiticreator.net/

91

Name _____ Date _____ Class _____

Who Is Creative? _____

Who Is the Person?	What Does He/She Do?	What Is Creative About It?

Seeing the World

Steven Herrick

Notes ▶
Observations ▶
Questions ▶

Every month or so,
when my brother and I
are bored with backyard games
and television, Dad says
"It's time to see the world."
So we climb the ladder to our attic,
push the window open,
and carefully, carefully,
scramble onto the roof.
We hang on tight as we scale the heights
to the very top.
We sit with our backs to the chimney
and see the world.
The birds flying
                    below us.
The trees swaying in the wind
                              below us.
Our cubbyhouse, meters
                        below us.
The distant city
                below us.
And then Dad, my brother, and I lie back
look up and watch
the clouds and sky
and dream
we're flying
we're flying.
In summer
with the sun and a gentle breeze
and not a sound anywhere
I'm sure I never want to land.

▶ SEEING THE WORLD

Steven Herrick

BEFORE READING

Why I Admire This Poem

I appreciate the wisdom of the dad in this poem. He sees that his young sons are bored and it's time to do something about that. He doesn't take them to the movies or to the arcade or even tell them to "run along and play." He knows they need a change of perspective, so he takes them on a perilous climb to the *very top* of the roof on their home. I also like what the dad does when he gets his sons to that perch. I should say that I like what he *doesn't* do. He doesn't try to point things out to them or ask a lot of questions about what they can see. He simply lets them observe *the world* of the title with *not a sound anywhere*. And I get the sense that they enjoy one another's company. That's the wisdom that I appreciate in the dad: he gives them the opportunity to get away from the world of *backyard games/and television* and see another world. What a wonderful gift!

Companion Poem

Just like this poem, Naomi Shihab Nye's "Every Cat Has a Story" is about seeing and imagining. The settings of the two poems are different, but take a look at how the poets look at life, how they find details all around them and make them come alive in a poem.

Special Words to Work Through

Steven Herrick is an Australian poet, and that will account for why he speaks of a *cubbyhouse* rather than a "club house," as Americans might, and why his measurement is in meters. Beyond that, take a look at some of the other words that he uses in his poem. When the trio is about to begin the climb, they *scramble onto the roof* and *hang on tight as we scale the heights*. I especially like the words *scramble* and *scale*. Uncommon words, but they convey these actions wonderfully.

FIRST READING: MEETING THE POEM

Ask your students how often they get bored. Can they name specific times when they were bored? They'll probably mention being bored during a class they don't like or when friends of their parents are around. Some will say they feel "bored"

THEMES, ISSUES, CONCEPTS

- fathers and sons
- sense of wonder
- contrast in poetry
- boredom

LITERARY TERMS

- mood
- images
- repetition
- line break
- hyperbole

ORGANIZERS

- Tone
- Sense Details

95

when they are by themselves. That's another area to explore: are they mostly bored when they are alone?

The other side of the equation is what your students do when they're bored. How do they manage to get through the boredom? Do they simply search out a friend? Do they have more inventive suggestions they can share with the others in the class? Don't be afraid to share your own thoughts and experiences with boredom.

CLOSE READING: GETTING TO KNOW THE POEM

One of the things I usually look for in a poem is contrast. I've noticed contrasts in a number of the poems in this book—in "Friends in the Klan," for example. In "Seeing the World" there is a contrast between the first five lines and the rest of the poem. From *bored with backyard games/and television* to *we're flying/we're flying* and *I'm sure I never want to land* is quite a contrast.

As is usually the case when contrast figures in a poem, there is a turning point—in this case, when the narrator tells us, *We sit with our backs to the chimney*. That is when he and his brother begin to notice how things are different from this unusual vantage point. The birds, the trees, the cubbyhouse, and the distant city all look different. This is a moment of growth in the narrator, when he sees things differently and is liberated from boredom. Now the things he sees—all things he can see from the ground as well—are different, and he is moved by the change in perspective. It's that liberation that lets him feel that they are flying.

Noticing Mood

How do your students feel when they read this poem? I suggested you ask your class this same question during your exploration of "Abandoned Farmhouse." Have your students use the **Tone in "Seeing the World"** organizer to help them write down their observations about how the poem makes them feel—note a couple of feelings they had while they were reading the poem and include a few specific details in the poem that made them feel that way.

My guess is they'll say the poem conveys a mood of contentment—*We sit with our backs to the chimney/and see the world*—and, later, joy—*we're flying/we're flying*. How does the poet create those feelings in the poem? He does it, of course, through the details he includes and his reaction to those details. (I have more to say about these details in the next section.)

Noticing Images

Herrick uses the senses to create images in this poem. He begins with the climb as they *scramble onto the roof*. From there, *We hang on tight as we scale the heights/to the very top*, until, *We sit with our backs to the chimney*. All of these actions rely on the sense of touch.

That changes in the next line as they *see the world* and he switches to the sense of sight. The narrator sees things *below us*: the birds flying, the trees swaying, the cubbyhouse, and the distant city.

See if your students can discover these as well as other images later in the poem. Give them the **Sense Details in "Seeing the World"** organizer and ask them to find some images in the poem and identify which sense each image appeals to. You might want to make a transparency of this organizer and add to it after your students have had the chance to fill theirs out individually.

Noticing Repetition

When a poet repeats a phrase in a poem he might be using that repetition to stitch the poem together. He may also repeat a word or phrase for emphasis. Herrick's repetitions fall into both categories. The trio scrambles onto the roof *carefully, carefully* because they are at *the very top* of the house. This is clearly a time for caution for the young roof climbers. The repetition of *below us* emphasizes how high they are, but it also conveys something of a sense of wonder, I think, when the narrator *realizes* how high they are. The birds are *below us*. The trees are *below us*. The cubbyhouse is *below us*. And the distant city is *below us*. With the final repetition—*we're flying/we're flying*—the narrator registers his awe at how high they are and what he can see from that height.

Noticing Line Breaks

This poem is another example of free verse that makes good use of line breaks. One way to check is to make a transparency of the poem and highlight the final word or two in each line. If Herrick has done his work, your highlighting should include most of the important words in the poem.

He uses another kind of line break trick when he writes:

> The birds flying
>   below us.
> The trees swaying in the wind
>   below us.
> Our cubbyhouse, meters
>   below us.
> The distant city
>   below us.

Not a conventional line break, is it? Besides emphasizing the *below us* phrase by repeating it, as we've already seen, he also does so by putting the phrases below the things to which they refer. Your students have probably used conventional line breaks in their own writing. In fact, most of the poems in this book use conventional line breaks. But the line breaks in "Seeing the World" might give your students the opportunity to look back over their own poems and see if there are alternative line breaks to the ones they used. Remind them that they need to have a reason for their line breaks, beyond *well, it looks cool this way*. Their reason should have something to do with the sense of their poem. Before you let your students try different line breaks, you might want to review the unit on line breaks on pages 24–25.

The line breaks in this poem are, in a sense, more important than they are in some other poems, because Herrick offers nearly no punctuation at the ends of lines to help us read the poem. But when we read the poem aloud, we can sense how to read the poem by where we pause for breath or make ever-so-slight pauses within a breath.

Noticing Hyperbole

Your students may recall that a hyperbole is an exaggeration. Sometimes the exaggeration is used for humor, but in this poem Herrick uses it, in *we're flying/we're flying*, to show the narrator's excitement and awe. Obviously, the trio on the roof of the house isn't literally flying. But it *feels* that way to them when they *lie back/look up and watch/the clouds and sky*.

AFTER READING: KNOWING THE POEM FOREVER

Say It Out Loud

How should you read this poem to convey the excitement the narrator feels? Because there are three people in the poem, I would work with a cast of three. The narrator of the poem would read the whole poem, assisted by the other two readers whenever the characters are doing something together. So I would have the narrator read the first four lines and then have the "Dad" character read line 5. Then have three voices read the section of the poem that begins *So we climb the ladder* until the second *we're flying*. At that point, the narrator can read the last four lines. Having him begin and end the poem solo is a nice way to bring it full circle.

Ask your students for alternative ways to present this poem. For example, this poem could be presented as a choral reading, but one that starts with a voice or two, then slowly adds voices as the excitement of the narrator builds.

Write About It

Have students explore one of these ideas in their writer's notebook:

1. Write about a time when you were so set in your ways that you never considered another way of looking at a situation or a person until something happened to change your thinking. Perhaps you judged a person by the way she dressed or the way he spoke the first time you met, until the two

of you had to work on a school project together. Make sure you give details about the original situation and why you felt the way you did, as well as the reason you changed your opinion.

2. Some people call once-in-a-lifetime experiences "peak experiences." Can you describe a peak experience you had? Try to capture the excitement of the moment the way Herrick does in "Seeing the World." Try to make sense impressions part of your description.

3. Consider playing with line breaks as another writing opportunity. Take a look at one of your poems and see if there is a different way to break up the lines. Does it make your poem different in any way? Is it easier to read? Play around with line breaks until you come up with something you like.

Issues/Themes/Topics

- Paying attention to the things around us
- Peak experiences
- Boredom
- Things you do with one parent but not the other
- Siblings

Related Poems

"To Look at Any Thing," by John Moffitt

"For Poets," by Al Young

"O I Have Dined on This Delicious Day," by Richard Snyder

"The Blue Between," by Kristine O'Connell George

"The Swing" by Robert L. Stevenson

Book Bridges

Here are three novels that explore the father-son relationship that Herrick writes about in his poem:

Lord of the Nutcracker Men by Iain Lawrence. A war story told by ten-year-old Johnny Briggs, whose father goes to fight in World War I. Johnny's attitude slowly changes from his enthusiasm for the toy soldiers his father carves in the trenches to an awareness of the waste of war.

My Dad's a Punk: 12 Stories About Boys and Their Fathers, edited by Tony Bradman. This collection of a dozen original stories explores the father-son relationship in a variety of situations. For older readers.

In Daddy's Arms I Am Tall: African Americas Celebrating Fathers, selected and illustrated by Javaka Steptoe. The collection celebrates the role of fathers in the African-American experience.

Online Resources

- Steven Herrick has a neat website: www.stevenherrick.com.au. Of course there are pictures and information about this Aussie poet, but my favorite part is the video section, where you can watch and listen to him reading five of his poems.

© 2011 by Paul B. Janeczko from *Reading Poetry in the Middle Grades*. Portsmouth, NH: Heinemann.

Name _____ Date _____ Class _____

Tone in "Seeing the World"

Feelings You Had	Details That Prompted These Feelings

Name _____ Date _____ Class _____

Sense Details in "Seeing the World" _____

Line	Details	Senses

© 2011 by Paul B. Janeczko from *Reading Poetry in the Middle Grades*. Portsmouth, NH: Heinemann.

Four Haiku

J. Patrick Lewis

Notes ▶
Observations ▶
Questions ▶

January woods—
a snowy owl *choo*ing one
  syllable of wind

  A spring peeper's song!
How strange to hear the echo
  of winter sleigh bells

A
red-
tailed
hawk
stalls
in tall
heat
above
the
wheat
kingdom

Thanksgiving Day—
Indian corn whispering
in the pilgrim cold

J. Patrick Lewis

BEFORE READING

Why I Admire These Poems

When students ask me how I started writing poetry, one of the things I tell them is that I wrote some haiku when I was in college. Even back then, I liked the form. Years later, as I began to read more about Buddhism, I made the connection between writing haiku and mindfulness, paying attention. When you write poetry, you need to pay attention, to look and listen for details, to be mindful with your senses. Throughout this book (as well as in my own poetry) I emphasize the importance of using sense details to create memorable images.

In haiku, however, the challenge is magnified because of the small canvas of seventeen syllables (give or take a syllable or two). The haiku poet needs to look beyond the loudness and complexity of the world and notice one small part of it, then capture it in words. Although young students consistently rank haiku high among their favorite poetic forms, this Japanese form may challenge some of your more literal-minded students because it requires readers to augment some of the details given by the poet. On the other hand, the form does allow readers a great opportunity to use their imagination to "fill in the blanks."

You can take advantage of the popularity of the haiku by supplying your students with samples of haiku that are accessible. For starters, check out the information I provide in the Book Bridges and Online Resources sections at the end of this unit. And because haiku are so short, you can easily write them on file cards and post a new one each day, perhaps near the light switch or below the classroom clock—someplace where your class will notice it.

Companion Poems

A number of poems in this book make good study companions: "Poppies," by Roy Scheele, and "When It Is Snowing," by Siv Cedering, are two. In addition, take another look at Naomi Shihab Nye's "Every Cat Has a Story" because of its short, imagistic stanzas.

THEMES, ISSUES, CONCEPTS

- really paying attention
- looking for details
- brevity

LITERARY TERMS

- sound
- haiku structure
- haiku elements

ORGANIZERS

- Haiku

Special Words to Work Through

There probably aren't any words in these haiku that your students wouldn't understand. However, there are a few details in them that you may need to explain or have your class explore online or in the library:

- Lewis uses "*choo*ing" in the first poem, which isn't a word at all but a play on *chewing one/syllable of wind*; it also mimics the "whooo" call of the snowy owl.

- A spring peeper is a small frog that announces spring—hence the name— in much of the eastern part of the United States, with, as Lewis observes, a sound like *winter sleigh bells*.

The Online Resources section includes links for information about and pictures of the spring peeper and the snowy owl.

FIRST READING: MEETING THE POEMS

After your class has read through these short poems, revisit the question, *what makes a good poem?* No doubt you and your students have already begun a list of the qualities you expect in a good poem. Ask whether these haiku prompt them to add anything to the list. They might bring up word choice, sense details, or economy of language. Even if these items are already on your list, it's good for students to see these qualities repeatedly appearing in poems. This discussion is also a good time to remind the class that a good poem need not be long.

CLOSE READING: GETTING TO KNOW THE POEMS

In addition to the brevity of haiku, I'm also impressed that they can be poetic without many of the elements of traditional poetry. Haiku do not have rhythm or rhyme and generally no metaphor, simile, or personification. Most of the time they capture a scene with a handful of simple words.

Most of your students will know that a haiku is written in seventeen syllables, arranged in three lines of five, seven, and five syllables. But here are a couple of other conventions that a haiku generally follows:

- It is written "in the moment"—in the present tense.

- It contains a seasonal word or reference. The reference could be direct, like *spring peeper*, or it can be indirect, like *the wheat kingdom*, referencing a crop growing in the summer.

- Generally, there is a slight pause at the end of the first or second line of a haiku. In a sense, the haiku therefore follows one of these configurations: five syllables/twelve syllables or twelve syllables/five syllables.

Although a haiku generally has a syllable count of five–seven–five, the syllable counts are guidelines rather than rules that can never be disregarded. It is more important that a haiku poet be faithful to the *spirit* of the form than a slave to five–seven–five.

I intentionally included Lewis' "red-tailed hawk" haiku because I wanted your students to see that haiku can be written in a form other than the traditional three-line format. Many of the books of haiku that I mention at the end of this unit feature poems that do not always adhere to the traditional three-line format. You can also find various haiku formats in my anthology of urban haiku called *Stone Bench in an Empty Park*, which is wonderfully illustrated with black-and-white photographs.

Noticing Details

To help your students explore these haiku, have them work in small groups on the **Haiku** organizer, which gives them the chance to zero in on key aspects of the poetic form: syllable count, seasonal reference, pause, and images. Because a haiku is a very quick snapshot, it needs sense details to create that vivid image. When your students have completed the organizer, give them a chance to discuss what details and images they've found in the poems.

For example, in the first haiku students might mention how the opening line—*January world*—appeals to our sense of sight, helping us picture a bleak landscape with trees that have lost their leaves. The remaining lines appeal to our sense of hearing: *a snowy owl* choo*ing one/syllable of wind*. We hear the sound of the owl's hoot. But *one/syllable of wind* also appeals to our sense of hearing, doesn't it?

Since the poems are short, your discussion of them may also be brief, but even a brief examination of each poem can lead your students to see the similarities and differences among them. You might create a matrix on the board to help your class organize their thoughts.

Noticing Sound

If you read these haiku carefully, you'll notice how Lewis plays with the sounds of words. In the third haiku, for example, can you hear the internal rhyme with *stalls* and *tall*, *heat*, and *wheat*? Then, too, there is the assonance—repetition of a vowel sound—of the *aw* sound in *hawk, stalls, tall*.

Lewis also uses words related to sound. I already mentioned the owl's sound in "*choo*ing." In the second haiku the key words—*song, echo, bells*—are related to sound. And let's not forget the *Indian corn whispering* in the last haiku. So not only do these haiku convey a vivid scene using details that appeal to the senses, they are also filled with the skillful use of sounds and sound words.

107

Noticing Structure

I mentioned earlier that a haiku generally has a slight pause either at the end of the first or second line. In three of Lewis's haiku the break is apparent because of punctuation that indicates a pause:

- *January woods—*
- *A spring peeper's song!*
- *Thanksgiving Day—*

The break in his other haiku isn't quite as apparent, but I think you can make a case for a pause after *hawk*. Ask your students what they think about a possible pause at that point in the poem. After several have weighed in on this question, ask some class members to read the haiku aloud. Does the oral reading influence their feelings about the pause?

AFTER READING: KNOWING THE POEMS FOREVER

Say It Out Loud

Because haiku are so short, they don't have the dramatic narrative force of a story poem or the give-and-take of a poem for two voices. Nonetheless, a series of haiku can make a compelling oral presentation in a way different from a longer poem.

To create a program of haiku, you'll need to find a number of them, perhaps twelve or fifteen, that you enjoy. There are some good ones at www.twodragon-flies.com. Your local public library probably has some books of haiku, such as:

Cricket Songs, by Harry Behn

Don't Step on the Sky: A Handful of Haiku, by Miriam Chaikin

In the Eyes of the Cat: Japanese Poetry for All Seasons, by Demi

One way to organize your poems is to present three or four for each season. Or you can feature haiku related to a favorite season.

Make sure that your presentation is simple, reflecting the simplicity of the form. Read the poems slowly, giving the audience a chance to focus on the details in the poem and the images they contain.

One last thing: there's nothing to stop you from writing your own haiku to present to the class. The best advice I can give you for writing your own haiku is: think small. Don't write a haiku about a hot summer day in the big city or a blizzard in New England. Way too big. Instead of writing about that New England blizzard, write about the snow piled on the bird feeder or on a swing in the playground. Write about that one bird you see trying to get at the seed in the feeder. See what I mean?

Write About It

Have students explore these ideas in their writer's notebook:

1. Bring the tips of your index fingers together. Then do the same thing with your thumbs so you get something that is close to a square. Hold that square at arm's length and look through it, as if it were the viewfinder of a camera. What do you see? Concentrate on what you see in that square. Slowly move that square, panning your yard or the street you live on. Pay attention to what you see in that window. When you find something that you think could be in a haiku, jot down your ideas.

2. Look again through that window. Pay attention. Do you notice other details to jot down? When you think you have enough notes, turn to a clean page in your writer's notebook and begin drafting your haiku.

Issues/Themes/Topics for Discussion

- Really paying attention
- The natural world
- Japanese haiku poets, like Issa and Basho

Related Poems

J. Patrick Lewis and I wrote two books of poems together, both related to haiku. *Wing Nuts: Screwy Haiku* is a collection of *senryu,* which is a Japanese form of poetry that follows the guidelines of haiku with one difference: instead of being about the natural world, senryu are about human nature (and therefore tend to be humorous). Senryu are great fun to read and write. Here's an example of a senryu that I wrote for that collection:

On Ferris wheel
I regret French fries, milkshake . . .
those below agree

Notice, by the way, that this poem has a five–seven–five syllable count, with a pause at the end of the second line.

The other book that we wrote is *Birds on a Wire: A Renga 'round Town. Renga* is a Japanese word that means *linked verse.* Renga are traditionally the work of two or more poets who take turns adding to the poem and playing off what the previous poet has written. As Pat said in the introduction to our book, "Like railroad cars in a line, each verse links in some way with the one preceding it, but not with the others."

Book Bridges

Haiku collections:

Today and Today, by Issa Kobayashi

Cricket Never Does, by Myra Cohn Livingston

One Leaf Rides the Wind, by Celeste Mannis

A Pocketful of Poems, by Nikki Grimes

Basho and the River Stones, by Tim Myers

If Not for the Cat, by Jack Prelutsky

Baseball Haiku: The Best Haiku Ever Written About the Game, edited by Cor Van Den Heuvel and Nanae Tamura

Dogku, by Andrew Clements

Strictly speaking, the last two books on the list do not contain haiku. Rather, they contain humorous poems that follow the five–seven–five syllable count.

Good books about writing haiku:

The Haiku Handbook, by William J. Higginson

The Essential Haiku, by Robert Hass

Haiku: A Poet's Guide, by Lee Gurga

How to Write Haiku and Other Short Poems, by Paul B. Janeczko

Online Resources

- Here is a source for information—including an audio loop!—about spring peepers: animals.nationalgeographic.com/animals/amphibians/spring-peeper.html.

- If you'd like to show your students a picture of a snowy owl, look here: www.allaboutbirds.org/guide/Snowy_Owl/id.

Name _____ Date _____ Class _____

Haiku

Haiku	Syllable Count	Seasonal Reference	Where Is Pause?	Images/Senses
January woods				
A spring peeper's song				
A red-tailed hawk				
Thanksgiving Day				

Tugboat at Daybreak

Lillian Morrison

The necklace of the bridge
is already dimmed for morning
but a tug in a tiara
glides slowly up the river,
a jewel of the dawn,
still festooned in light.

The river seems to slumber
quiet in its bed,
as silently the tugboat,
a ghostlike apparition,
moves twinkling up the river
and disappears from sight.

Notes ▶
Observations ▶
Questions ▶

From *Reading Poetry in the Middle Grades*. Portsmouth, NH: Heinemann. © 1992 by Lillian Morrison from *Whistling the Morning In*. Reprinted by permission of Wordsong, an imprint of Boyds Mills Press.

▶ TUGBOAT AT DAYBREAK

Lillian Morrison

▌BEFORE▐ READING

Why I Admire This Poem

Images are the sensations poets build with their words using their senses. For example, in "Tugboat at Daybreak" Morrison uses *glides*, a word that appeals to the sense of touch, in that it connotes the sensation of movement, something we can feel, although not with our hands. It also connotes calm. A swan glides. A parasail glides.

When a poem connects with readers, it's usually because they *feel* something as they read it. It might be empathy for the narrator or for a character in a poem. Dr. Carver in "Friends in the Klan," for example. However, while we admire the courage of Dr. Carver, we feel outrage at the way African Americans were treated. We also tune in to the mood of a poem, a feeling the poet arouses with the words she chooses and the images she creates with those words. The mood of a poem is often subtle, as is true in "Tugboat at Daybreak."

Companion Poems

This poem creates a vivid scene. You can compare it with the scenes created by "Abandoned Farmhouse," "Deserted Farm," "Poppies," and "When It Is Snowing." Ask your students to compare the details and the *types* of details that these poets use and the senses to which they appeal.

Special Words to Work Through

It's important that your student know what *tiara* means, because it fits in with the other jewel-related words in the first stanza. Two other words that students need to understand but that may be unfamiliar are *festooned* and *apparition*. These words all contribute to the overall image Morrison creates in this poem.

▌FIRST▐ READING: **MEETING THE POEM**

Ask your students what they think of when they hear the word *image*. Write some of their replies on the board. They will likely mention something visual, perhaps a painting or a photograph. To get them to recognize that the images in poetry can appeal to many senses, hand out copies of the **Senses** organizer. The five senses are listed across the tops of the columns. Below each is a space for students to write words and phrases that appeal to that sense. For example, for taste, they could write

THEMES, ISSUES, CONCEPTS

• scene in poetry
• observing

LITERARY TERMS

• setting
• image
• details
• mood
• metaphor

ORGANIZERS

• Senses

113

words like *sour, sweet, bitter, salty*. Or they could also include specific tastes like *blueberry, peppermint, lemon*. The point of the exercise is to help students think in terms of words that appeal to *all* their senses.

After the students have worked with this organizer individually, ask them to share their ideas with the class as you record their responses on the board or on chart paper. Make sure you point out that a word can have more meanings than its obvious one. It can be used metaphorically. For example, a victory in a game can be *sweet*, and a last-second defeat can leave a *bitter taste* in your mouth. The wonderful words we have at our disposal can be used in many different ways.

CLOSE READING: GETTING TO KNOW THE POEM

Through discussion, invite students to share what they notice about the poem. Do any of them notice that it is a poem of contrasts? Lillian Morrison describes a blue-collar tugboat, the workhorse of the harbor, in the quiet of dawn, but the boat does nothing to disrupt the quiet scene. Rather than describing the roaring diesel engine, she features the lights on the bridge (a *necklace*) and the lights on the boat (*a tug in a tiara*) and sees the hard-working boat as *a jewel of the dawn/still festooned in light*.

The focus in the second stanza shifts to sound, or rather the absence of it. Once again there is a contrast between the loud noises most people expect to hear from a tugboat and the quiet scene Morrison describes. The river *seems to slumber/quiet in its bed*. The tugboat moves *silently . . . a ghostlike apparition* before it *disappears from sight*.

Noticing Sense Details

Ask a couple of students to read "Tugboat at Daybreak" aloud. After the students have heard the poem read aloud, ask them to write the names of the five senses in the white space surrounding the poem. Tell them to spread the words out, because they are going to highlight all the words and phrases in the poem that appeal to their senses, then draw lines from these words and phrases to the appropriate sense labels.

Remind your students that some words might appeal to more than one sense. For example, *glides* could appeal to the sense of touch (how it feels to glide) as well as to the sense of sight (as you see something glide by). Students also need to know that a poet might not appeal to all the senses in any one poem. Suggest that they concentrate on what is actually in the poem, without overthinking or overexamining the words and images.

Noticing Mood

After your students have carefully considered the sense details in "Tugboat at Daybreak," they are ready to discuss the mood created by these images. If I had to describe the mood this poem creates, I would probably say *tranquil*. In the first stanza the lights of the bridge are *already dimmed for morning*, which is generally a quiet time of day. And the tugboat *glides slowly up the river*. The tugboat is a *jewel of the dawn/still festooned in light*. No mention of any sounds from the boat. We have a dawn scene devoid of sound.

This quiet mood is reinforced in nearly every line of the second stanza:

The river seems to slumber
quiet in its bed,
as silently the tugboat,
a ghostlike apparition,
moves twinkling up the river
and disappears from sight.

Note the soft, gentle words and phrases: *slumbers, quiet in its bed, silently, ghostlike, twinkling, disappears*. That said, this is my own particular case: students can make compelling cases for other related moods—encourage them to! The key is to have them support their ideas by pointing to specific words and lines. Serene, solitary, soothing—there is no one most correct mood.

Noticing Figurative Language

As part of the discussion of the images Morrison uses to create a mood, you need to recognize her use of figurative language as a way of creating those images. For example, she uses metaphors in a number of spots in the first stanza. First she refers to the lights on the bridge as a *necklace*. Two lines later she sees the boat with its lights as *a tug in a tiara*. Finally, she refers to the tugboat as *a jewel of the dawn*.

Your students may also notice Morrison's use of personification in the opening two lines of the second stanza: *The river seems to slumber/quiet in its bed*. I'll bet Morrison chuckled over her play on the words *river* and *bed*.

Morrison uses these bits of figurative language to create an image of the lighted tugboat in the first stanza and to reinforce the feeling of calm in the second stanza. It's a good idea to point out how Morrison uses these techniques to good purpose in her poem—she's not merely tossing in some metaphors for metaphor's sake.

AFTER READING: KNOWING THE POEM FOREVER

Say It Out Loud

This is such a hushed poem of only two stanzas that it seems best performed by a single reader. Yet, because it does have two stanzas, you could have each read by a different reader. A third possibility is to break the poem into a number of logical parts. Both stanzas can be nicely divided into three sections of two lines each. You might be able to dress up your performance a bit by adding a strand or two of clear Christmas lights as the *necklace of the bridge*.

Write About It

Have students explore one of these ideas in their writer's notebook:

1. Each stanza of "Tugboat at Daybreak" is similar to a haiku, in that it focuses on a very limited scene, with a limited amount of action. Can you think of a couple of scenes that you can describe in rich details like the ones Lillian Morrison uses? Go on an "observation walk," notebook in hand, ready to jot down details, perhaps comparisons that come to mind to describe the various scenes you observe. Take your time. Stop to pay attention. As you observe and take notes, don't forget to bring your other senses into the mix. Of course you will be looking, but that shouldn't stop you from listening or touching as well.

2. Write a version of this poem that is the opposite of Morrison's. Imagine the potential noise of the scene with the volume turned way up. Or maybe you capture the scene at rush hour, the bridge leading to a major city. What else might you change in your version of the poem? What about the lights on the bridge? What about the narrator?

3. Write a poem about a different scene. You could describe a nature area or a city square at midnight or dawn—that sort of thing. Your poem needn't be longer than "Tugboat at Daybreak." Include just a few details in each stanza.

Issues/Themes/Topics for Discussion

- The quiet of nature
- The senses
- Observation
- Noticing

Related Poems

Lillian Morrison delights in word play. But she also enjoys writing about sports. Among her books of sports poems are:

At the Crack of the Bat: Baseball Poems

Way to Go!: Sports Poems

Slam Dunk: Basketball Poems

The Break Dance Kids: Poems of Sport, Motion, and Locomotion

To find more about her and her books, you can check out these websites:

- www.jacketflap.com/persondetail.asp?person=94497

- www.librarything.com/author/morrisonlillian

- www.biblio.com/author_biographies/2272743/Lillian_Morrison.html

Book Bridges

It would be interesting to see how other poets handle something as elusive as fog. Some use it as the subject of a poem, whereas others use it a part of the setting. Of course, you can start with Carl Sandburg's classic, "Fog." He wrote other poems in which fog is featured: "Fog Portrait," "Pearl Fog," and "Baltic Fog Notes" are worth reading. Other poems to consider are:

- "Fog," by Amy Clampitt

- "Fog" and "Boats in a Fog," by Robinson Jeffers

- "Gray Fog," by Sara Teasdale

- "Fog," by Emma Lazarus

Online Resources

- en.wikipedia.org/wiki/Tugboat is a great starting point for information about tugboats. It explains the types of tugboats and tugboat propulsion. My favorite page is the gallery of tugboat photographs.

- If you want to see tugboats at play, go to gcaptain.com/maritime/blog/the-race-is-on-nyc-tugboat-photos for pictures and explanation of the Great Tugboat Race in New York Harbor. It includes a YouTube link.

Name _____ Date _____ Class _____

Senses _____

Sight	Sound	Smell	Taste	Touch

Ode to Family Photographs

Gary Soto

This is the pond, and these are my feet.
This is the rooster, and this is more of my feet.

Mama was never good at pictures.

This is a statue of a famous general who lost an arm,
And this is me with my head cut off.

This a trash can chained to a gate,
This is my father with his eyes half-closed.

This a photograph of my sister
And a giraffe looking over her shoulder.

This is our car's front bumper.
This is a bird with a pretzel in its beak.
This is my brother Pedro standing on one leg on a rock,
With a smear of chocolate on his face.

Mama sneezed when she looked
Behind the camera: the snapshots are blurry,
The angles dizzy as a spin on a merry-go-round.

But we had fun when Mama picked up the camera.
How can I tell?
Each of us laughing hard.
Can you see: I have candy in my mouth.

Notes ▶
Observations ▶
Questions ▶

▶ ODE TO FAMILY PHOTOGRAPHS

Gary Soto

BEFORE READING

Why I Admire This Poem

There are a number of things I like about this poem. For one thing, it's celebratory. Although you expect a sense of celebration in an ode, Soto's ode bursts with energy. I also like it because it portrays a joyous family relationship. What I like even more is that the poem celebrates imperfection! True, it's about family photographs, but it's really about the enjoyment the narrator finds in Mama's botched photographs: of just his feet, with his head cut off, the front bumper of the car. These photographs bring joy to the young narrator. How can we tell? Easy: *Each of us laughing hard./Can you see? I have candy in my mouth*. Rather than make fun of Mama, the narrator embraces the memories in these photographs, and the woman who took them.

Companion Poem

This poem could be used in conjunction with "Abandoned Farmhouse." Both poems capture a family essence, but where something has gone *terribly wrong* for the farm family, the family in this poem enjoys the silliness of Mama's flawed photographs. Can your students feel the difference in the mood of each poem? This point of comparison could prompt an interesting class discussion.

Possible Ways to Introduce the Poem

As he does with most of his poems, Gary Soto uses simple language to create his images and describe the action, so your students should have no trouble with the vocabulary. Since the poem is about family photographs, you might ask your students to notice the *things* in the poem, especially in the first twelve lines or so. What nouns does Soto use in this part of the poem?

In the Write About It section later in this unit, I suggest that the students use some of their own family photos as an aid in writing an ode of their own. But at this point in the unit, you might ask the students to look through their photos and identify the *things* in their photos, the way Soto does in his poem. This might help the students notice the essence of their photographic images. It can also help them feel more confident if you ask them to write their own ode to family photographs.

THEMES, ISSUES, CONCEPTS

- Latino poet
- family
- memories
- ritual

LITERARY TERMS

- images
- mood
- patterns
- structure

ORGANIZERS

- Ode Topics
- Visual Images Album
- Patterns/Repetition

121

FIRST READING: MEETING THE POEM

Can we be okay with imperfection? Or must everything be perfect for us to feel content or happy? It seems that this poem raises this issue. Why not ask your students these questions before they read the poem? Another point to consider is whether disappointment is connected to the expectations others place on us or to those we place on ourselves. Can they name areas in their lives where they are expected by family or friends to be perfect? Do expectations of perfection create stress in their lives? How do they deal with these expectations? Ask your students to think of a time like that in the poem, a time when they were able to accept imperfection with good cheer.

CLOSE READING: GETTING TO KNOW THE POEM

The ode is a poem of celebration. When the ancient Greeks wrote odes, they followed a strict form in three parts. But as the years passed, the formal structure of the ode disappeared (although it enjoyed a revival in seventeenth-century England). Poets felt that they could write odes without being restricted by iambic pentameter (a line of poetry with ten syllables, with a stress on syllables 2, 4, 6, 8, 10) and a rhyme scheme of *ababcdecde*. Soto's "Ode to Family Photographs" is a free verse poem with stanzas and lines of varying lengths.

Since the ode has been freed from the restrictions of the ancients, you might want to consider having your students write an ode to something they celebrate. You can get an idea of suitable topics from some of the things Latino poet Soto writes about in *Neighborhood Odes*: "Ode to La Tortilla," "Ode to the Sprinkler," "Ode to Pomegranates," and "Ode to Weight Lifting." Another renowned writer of odes was Pablo Neruda, who seemed partial to writing odes to food. In his book *Ode to Common Things*, he writes poems to bread, soap, a bed, and a box of tea. Give your students a copy of the **Ode Topics** organizer and ask them to write some specific details about what they would say in praise of an object or person.

An ode is a natural poetic form to combine with a piece of art, like a photograph or a painting of the object the ode is celebrating. When mounted on construction paper alongside the poem, the resulting collages could make up an impressive "ode wall" in your classroom.

Noticing Images

This poem is filled with images, but, as you would expect in a poem about photographs, they are visuals images, things we see in the photographs. Distribute the **Visual Images Album** organizer and ask your students to identify some of the visual images they discovered in Soto's verbal photograph album. The organizer provides space for a dozen images. Make sure students list the details in the images. Because images can appeal to different senses, ask your students to note as well any images that appeal to one of their other senses.

Noticing Mood

By the third line—*Mama was never good at pictures*—we know that this is a playful poem: we recognize the kindness in the statement. But there are hints in the first two lines, both of which end with photos of the narrator's feet! Can your students see the playfulness in the third stanza with the lighthearted contrast between the *famous general who lost an arm* and *me/with my head cut off*? (I wonder if the general lost his arm in battle or only in Mama's photograph.) Have students point out other details in the poem that help create the playful mood.

Noticing Patterns

Students probably know that rhyming poems follow a pattern, which includes rhythm and rhyme, and perhaps stanza form as well, as in "A Poison Tree." On the other hand, one of the things that makes free verse "free" is the absence of patterns of rhythm and rhyme. However, that's not to say that there are no patterns (or near patterns) in free verse.

Divide your class into groups of two or three students each. Distribute copies of the **Patterns/Repetitions** organizer. Ask the groups to read "Ode to Family Photographs," looking for any patterns or repetitions. Remind them that the patterns need not run through the entire poem. For example, half of the lines in the poem begin with the same phrase, *This is* (or *And this is*). That phrase is part of the pattern of the poem, one of the things that gives the poem its rhythm, even though this is free verse. Your students may also notice the structure of the lines in the middle of the poem, which follow this pattern: *This is* [noun] [modifier/description/detail], as in *This is me with my head cut off.* A free verse poet uses strategies like these to unify his poem, to make it hang together.

Noticing Structure

As your students have already discovered, much of the poem is a list of various "flawed" family photographs. The list is interrupted by two sections (line 3 and lines 14–16) in which the narrator comments on how inept Mama is with a camera.

However, the poem changes direction in line 17 with the word *but*. The final four lines of the poem say, in effect, that even though Mama took many silly photographs, it doesn't matter because *we had fun when Mama picked up a camera.*

AFTER READING: **KNOWING THE POEM FOREVER**

Say It Out Loud

"Ode to Family Photographs" can benefit from some props during a reading. I can picture a student riffling through a handful of photographs, looking at one before reading each *this is* statement. Perhaps other students can mime each scene. I can even imagine a flash going off whenever the narrator flips to a new photograph! When the reader gets to line 14, he can look at the audience as he recites the rest of the poem, perhaps flashing the picture where he's *laughing hard* and showing the candy in his mouth.

Can your students think of any other ways of presenting this poem? Can any of your students recite it in Spanish?

Write About It

Have students explore one of these ideas in their writer's notebook:

1. Bring in several photographs of yourself and your family when you were younger, taken at places and events you remember fondly. Using "Ode to Family Photographs" as a model, write a list poem based on these photographs. Your list poem need not be humorous like Soto's. You might write more of a "documentary" list poem, or perhaps a travelogue.

2. Is there someone in the photographs who is no longer part of your family? Perhaps someone has died or left after a divorce. Perhaps you want to take care of some unfinished business with that person. Write a letter to her or him, explaining some of the things that have happened since she/he left. You can also write a poem of address to that person.

3. How else can the photos serve as a springboard to a piece of writing? You could write a description of a person shown in one of them. Or a short narrative connected to a photograph. Is there any sort of mystery connected to one of the persons in a photo? Can you explain that mystery? Offer a solution to it?

Issues/Themes/Topics for Discussion

- Family
- Memories
- Rituals
- Celebrations
- Myths
- Mysteries

Related Poems

Gary Soto writes very accessible poems, including five books that are written for young readers, which are listed at his website: www.garysoto.com/poetry.html

You can find most of Soto's poems for adults at the Chronicle Books website: www.chroniclebooks.com/index/store,books

Love to Mamá: A Tribute to Mothers, edited by Pat Mora, is a wonderful collection of work by Hispanic poets, among them Judith Ortiz Cofer, Tony Median, and Mora herself.

Book Bridges

More by Gary Soto:

In addition to his poetry, Soto has written quite a few novels and books of short stories. They are all listed on his website, but here are a few direct links:

- short stories: www.garysoto.com/short_stories.html
- novels for ages 10–14: www.garysoto.com/novels.html
- poetry for ages 10–14: www.garysoto.com/poetry.html

Fiction:

The Seer of Shadows, by Avi. A young photographer's apprentice in 1872 New York uncovers a fraudulent spirit photography racket and accidentally frees the real host of a dead girl bent on revenge.

Journey, by Patricia MacLachlan. When their mother goes off and leaves her two children with their grandparents, they feel as if their past has been erased until Grandfather finds a way to restore it.

Nonfiction:

The Mexican American Family Album by Dorothy and Thomas Hoobler. Although this book does include information about high-profile Mexican Americans, like Cesar Chavez, it focuses on the everyday experiences of unknown Mexican immigrants.

Online Resources

- If you'd like to incorporate a photography project in connection with studying this poem but aren't sure where to start, take a look at the work done by the students at the University of Chicago Laboratory School: www.ucls.uchicago.edu/students/projects/index.aspx.

- If your students have access to a digital camera and Adobe Photoshop Elements, you can find lots of student projects and examples of student work at: www.adobe.com/education/instruction/adsc/#impressionist

125

Name _____ Date _____ Class _____

Ode Topics _____

Subject of Ode

Details

_____
_____
_____
_____
_____
_____
_____
_____
_____
_____
_____
_____
_____
_____
_____
_____
_____
_____
_____
_____
_____

Name _____ Date _____ Class _____

Visual Images Album

Name _____ Date _____ Class _____

Patterns/Repetitions in "Ode to Family Photographs" _____

Read the poem again and see if you notice any patterns, such as words and phrases that are repeated throughout the poem. Patterns need not occur in every line.

<table>
<tr><td>What words begin many of the first twelve lines?</td></tr>
</table>

<table>
<tr><td>Many of the first twelve lines follow this pattern: This is (noun) (modifier/description/action). For example, This is the pond in the first line.
Write out the lines and parts of lines in the poem that follow this pattern:</td></tr>
</table>

© 2011 by Paul B. Janeczko from Reading Poetry in the Middle Grades. Portsmouth, NH: Heinemann.

Hoods

Paul B. Janeczko

Notes ▶
Observations ▶
Questions ▶

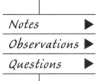

In black leather jackets,
watching Spider work
the wire coat hanger
into Mrs. Koops car,
they reminded me of crows
huddled around a road kill.
Startled,
they looked up,
then back
as Spider,
who nodded once,
setting them free
toward me.
I bounded away,
used a parking meter
to whip me around the corner
past Janelli's Market,
the darkened Pine Street Grille,
and the steamed windows
of Sudsy's Modern Laundromat.
I climbed—two at a time—
the granite steps
of the Free Public Library
and pushed back thick wooden doors
as the pursuing pack stopped—
sinners at the door of a church.

From the corner table of the reference room
I watched them
pacing,
head turning every time the door opened,
pacing,
until Spider arrived
to draw them away.
I waited,
fingering hearts,
initials carved into the table,
grinning as I heard myself telling Raymond
of my death-defying escape.

▶ **HOODS**

Paul B. Janeczko

BEFORE READING

What Sparked This Poem

Because my first two books of poems—*Brickyard Summer* and *Stardust otel*—were written in first person, many readers took them for autobiography. But these poems are not the story of my life when I was a teenager. Far from it. Trust me. My life at that point was far too boring to interest anyone. However, like most writers, I did mine my past for characters, scenes, and events that I could use to grow a poem.

The kernel of my history that I used in this poem was the narrator's antagonist, Spider. He is based on my older brother, who was, well, a lot like Spider. Beyond that character, however, the poem is fiction: the narrative is made up, as are the setting and, of course, the narrator.

All of this is a reminder that your students need to understand that the narrator of a poem is not automatically the poet. Sometimes it's obvious that the narrator *is* the poet, but at other times it might not be so clear. Remind your students to take the narrator of a poem to be a voice separate from the author unless and until they discover otherwise.

Companion Poem

The narrator in this poem and the one in "Ode to Family Photographs," by Gary Soto, speak in a similar adolescent-male voice. Ask your students what they learn about these two narrators from how the act, what they say, and how they say it. Would they like to be friends with either or both of them? Do they know someone like them? Is there something they like about them from these poems?

Special Language to Work Through

The language in this poem is pretty simple, so I doubt that your students will have any trouble with it. However, they may be more apt to think of a "hood" as a place rather than a person. You can tell them that *hood* is a shortened form of *hoodlum*, meaning a tough guy or a thug. "Hoods" is from *Brickyard Summer,* a book of poems I wrote with a narrator who is never named, so you might need to explain that context to your class. Two other characters in the book appear in this poem. Spider is one of the narrator's antagonists, and Raymond is the narrator's best friend.

THEMES, ISSUES, CONCEPTS

- action-reaction in poetry
- bullies/bullying
- story poem

LITERARY TERMS

- plot
- metaphor
- simile
- line breaks
- images
- hyperbole

ORGANIZERS

- Action-Reaction

FIRST READING: MEETING THE POEM

Spider is a bully, or at least someone who likes to intimidate others. Ask your students what they picture when they hear the word *bully*. Does your school have a program to deal with bullying? If so, perhaps you could invite a counselor to your class to discuss bullying with the students. Write some characteristics of bullies on the board. Have they ever had an encounter with a bully? Who was the bully? Can they recall specific details about the bully—how he spoke or how he dressed? What were the circumstances of the encounter? Did the bully act alone? Why did they incur the wrath of the bully? Did they do something, or did the bully pick on them simply because he could?

The other side of the coin is whether any of them have acted as bullies. What did your students learn from their experience as bully or victim?

CLOSE READING: GETTING TO KNOW THE POEM

I like to think of "Hoods" as a poem of action/reaction. The narrative begins with an action and a reaction, which leads to another action. Distribute copies of the **Action–Reaction** organizer and ask your students to write the initial action of the poem in the first box. In the box to the right, write in a reaction that comes from that initial action. Ask them to fill in the other boxes with similar actions and reactions. They will probably come up with some of these ideas:

- Action: At the start of the poem, the narrator spots the boys breaking into a car.

- Reaction: Spider sends his accomplices after the narrator.

- Reaction: The narrator flees to the reference room of the public library, where he observes the danger lurking on the street. It might be interesting to think here about why the place of refuge is the library.

- Action: The gang's leader arrives *to draw them away*.

- Reaction: The narrator basks in the satisfaction of having eluded the "hoods," with a further bonus that he can brag about it to his best friend, Raymond.

Noticing Plot

Although "Hoods" has only two stanzas, there are a few turning points in the narrative action. Each one begins with the narrator telling what he did next: *I bounded away, I climbed, I watched, I waited.* Each phrase propels the narrator into a new stage of his escape.

On the board, draw a plot line, with its rising action line, climax peak, and falling action line (see Figure 5).

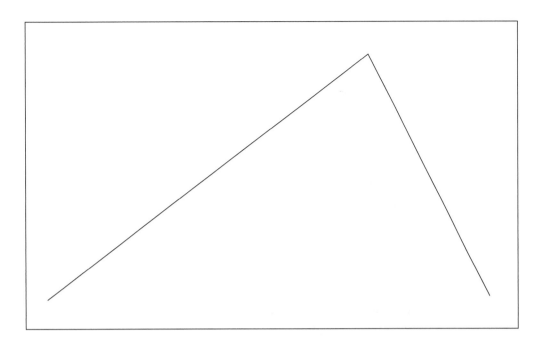

Figure 5

Ask your students to supply information that maps the action of the narrative. Where do the four turning points mentioned above fall on the plot line?

Noticing Figurative Language

Your students will know by now the difference between a simile (a comparison using *like* or *as*) and a metaphor (a direct comparison). While I do not use much figurative language in the poem, I do use a couple of comparisons to create an image for the reader. Early in the poem, I compare the boys in *black leather jackets* to *crows/huddled around a road kill*. And at the end of the first stanza, I wanted to show how abruptly the boys stopped at the door of the library by using a metaphor comparing the boys to *sinners at the door of a church*. I use both of these comparisons so the reader can *see* the scene. (See also Noticing Images, on the next page. When you discuss images, remind your students that the term is not strictly a visual one. Images in poems can appeal to other senses.)

Noticing Line Breaks

In discussions of other poems, I've spoken of the fundamentals of line breaks in free verse, how the words on a line need to feel as if they belong together. When I wrote "Hoods," I tried to follow that "rule." But because I wanted this poem to be a poem of suspense and action, I used a number of short lines in the hope of prolonging that suspense and creating a sense of breathlessness. For example, take a look at lines 7–13:

Startled,
they looked up,

133

then back
at Spider,
who nodded once,
setting them free
toward me.

I did a similar thing in the second stanza, twice using *pacing* by itself to build suspense. I put *I waited* by itself for the same reason.

As you discuss the line breaks in this poem, ask your students to take a close look at the words I put at the end of the lines. They should be the more important words in the poem. Do you think they are?

Noticing Images

As I worked on this poem, I pictured a chase scene in a movie, so I wanted to make sure my readers could see characters propelling the action in a particular setting. I set the scene with boys *in black leather jackets* gathered around a car like *crows/huddled around a road kill*. I use the black of the jackets and the crows, as well as the image of scavenger crows picking at a dead animal, to create a sense of danger. The spell is broken with *startled/they looked up*. Once again I use an action that the reader can *see*.

With the nod from Spider, the chase is on. I include the names of stores the narrator races by as well as the senses of sight and touch as he uses *a parking meter/to whip me around the corner*. Then he hurriedly climbs the steps of the library *two at a time*. The stanza ends with him safely in the library, the hoods outside like *sinners at the door of a church*. All details, I hope, that the reader can *see*.

The scene of the second stanza is the reference room, where the narrator, nervous from the chase, watches the gang waiting for him. Luckily for him, at least for now, Spider arrives and calls off his gang. In the final five lines of the poem, I wanted to slow down the action, so I had the narrator *fingering hearts,/initials carved into the table*, working this time with the sense of touch, but still trying to create an image.

Noticing Hyperbole

While your students may not know this term, they certainly know what it means to exaggerate, which is what this term means. I use hyperbole in the final stanza of the poem, when the narrator has successfully eluded the gang of "hoods" that was chasing him. They are no longer hovering at the door of the library waiting for him. The narrator, relaxed by this turn of events, imagines what he'll tell his best friend, Raymond. Of course, he intends to embellish the story, which I chose to show with hyperbole when the narrator grins as he *heard myself telling Raymond/of my death-defying escape*.

AFTER READING: KNOWING THE POEM FOREVER

Say It Out Loud

Because this is a poem about action with a single narrator, it strikes me as a poem for a single reader. However, the narrator's tale could be enhanced by some pantomimed actions. Perhaps the scene could unfold behind the reader or even around him. You and your class might get some ideas about how to stage this action poem by watching the clashes between the Jets and the Sharks in *West Side Story*.

Write About It

Have students explore one of these ideas in their writer's notebook:

1. Write about an encounter you had with a bully. Who was the bully? Can you recall specific details about the bully—how he or she spoke or dressed? What were the circumstances of the encounter? Did the bully act alone? Why did you incur the wrath of the bully? Did you do something, or did the bully pick on you simply because he could?

2. Or write about a time when *you* were the bully. Was it in a physical way, by pushing or shoving or fighting? Or maybe you were a bully with your words and your attitude. Why do you think you acted that way?

3. What did you learn from your experience as bully or victim?

4. Write about a time when you embellished or exaggerated your achievements or skills. What were the circumstances? Were you trying to impress someone? Trying to avoid getting into trouble? Were your embellishments believed or were your exaggerations unmasked? What did that feel like?

Issues/Themes/Topics for Discussion

- Bullies and bullying
- Tall tales

Related Poems

"Spider," the poem that immediately follows "Hoods" in *Brickyard Summer;* if you and your students are curious about what happens to the bully, read this poem (The book is filled with the further adventures of the nameless narrator.)

"Blubber Lips," by Jim Daniels

135

Book Bridges

Fiction:

Belling the Tiger, by Mary Stolz. Bob and Ozzie are mice, and brothers. Their job is to slip a bell around the neck of the cat. This novel is about realizing that the bullies you need to face aren't quite so tough. It's also a book about the value of best friends.

Bad Girls, by Cynthia Voigt. Mikey and Margalo meet in Mrs. Chemsky's fifth-grade classroom and team up. They so effectively deal with the class bully, Louis Caselli, that his resulting rage gets him expelled from school. Like the characters in the book, this one's best for fifth grade and up.

Carlos Is Gonna Get It, by Kevin Emerson. Trina and her seventh-grade friends hatch a plan to teach a disruptive boy classmate a lesson, but Trina has second thoughts. Paints a realistic picture of the bullying and interpersonal dramas of middle school.

Slake's Limbo, by Felice Holman. Thirteen-year-old Aremis Slake flees into the subway tunnels of New York, and he intends never to leave.

Nonfiction:

Gangs, by Laurie Willis. A exploration of gangs, including their appeal, the difficulties of leaving a gang, and their impact on families and on society in general.

Online Resources

- *West Side Story*, the 1961 musical, is readily available on DVD. In addition, some scenes are available on YouTube.

Name _____ Date _____ Class _____

Action-Reaction in "Hoods"

Action   **Reaction**

FRIENDS IN THE KLAN
1923

Marilyn Nelson

Black veterans of WWI experienced
such discrimination in veterans' hospitals
that the Veterans' Administration, to save face,
opened Tuskegee, a brand-new hospital
for Negroes only. Under white control.
(White nurses, who were legally excused
from touching blacks, stood holding their elbows
and ordering colored maids around, white shoes
tapping impatiently.)
             The Professor joined
the protest. When the first black doctor arrived
to jubilation, the KKK uncoiled
its length and hissed. *If you want to stay alive
be away Tuesday*. Unsigned. But a familiar hand.
The Professor stayed. And he prayed for his friend in the Klan.

Notes ▶

Observations ▶

Questions ▶

Marilyn Nelson

BEFORE READING

Why I Admire This Poem

I admit that when I saw the title of this poem in *Carver, A Life in Poems*, by Marilyn Nelson, I did a double take. "Friends" and "Klan" didn't seem to belong in the same phrase, especially when used as a title for a poem about George Washington Carver, the revered African American teacher and leader. Could Carver be friends with someone in a hateful racist organization? But Nelson lets her story play out in the poem, until we understand the significance of those two words in the title.

"Friends in the Klan," it turns out, is a poem about courage. More important, however, it is a poem about a man who *showed* his courage for all to see. Not only did Carver stand up to the bigots in Tuskegee, he prays for *his friend in the Klan*, the one who sent him a letter threatening his life. Now, *that* is real courage.

Companion Poems

It might make an interesting lesson to compare the way Carver responds to a bully to the way the narrator in "Hoods" responds. Sure, the stakes are much greater in "Friends in the Klan," but the notion of how to respond to a bully runs through both poems. And let's not forget the intolerant speaker 1 in Janet S. Wong's "Speak Up," who tries to bully the other speaker in the poem.

Special Language to Work Through

Although the language in the poem is fairly simple, some of your students may need help with a few words, like *discrimination*, *jubilation*, and *veteran*. Beyond vocabulary issues, your students will also need some help understanding the historical era in which the poem takes place. Such an exploration is an excellent opportunity for your students to research appropriate topics. Perhaps you can work with a social studies teacher.

Besides the historical reality of racial discrimination in the United States, here are a few other areas your students can investigate to give them a clearer understanding of the situation in "Friends in the Klan":

- Background on the work of the Veterans Administration, the agency designed to care for soldiers who were returning in great numbers from World War I. Although the agency is now called the Department of Veteran Affairs, it does much the same work it did since it was dedicated on Lincoln's birthday in 1923, consolidating a number of government agencies.

THEMES, ISSUES, CONCEPTS

- African American poet
- bullies
- courage
- history in poetry
- contrast in poetry
- racism
- civil rights movement

LITERARY TERMS

- images
- figurative language
- metaphor
- structure
- repetition

ORGANIZERS

- What Is Courage?

139

- The KKK, in order to understand the fear that its chapters instilled in many communities.
- The Tuskegee hospital.

A few helpful websites are included under Online Resources.

FIRST READING: MEETING THE POEM

The story presented in this poem raises a number of questions that are worthwhile asking and discussing with your class. The **What Is Courage?** organizer can help groups of two or three students stay focused as they discuss the following questions:

- What is courage?
- Must it be physical?
- Who are two people (people you know, fictional characters, people from the news) who have courage?
- Why do you think these people are courageous?
- What qualities do these people show?

When the groups have had time to consider the questions, ask someone from each group to present a report to the class. Write the important points of their responses on the board. Can you and your students see any similarities in these responses?

CLOSE READING: GETTING TO KNOW THE POEM

This is a poem of contrasts between black and white people as seen in the treatment of the *Black veterans of WWI* and the attitudes of the white management of the Veterans Administration. The black veterans are given a *brand-new hospital*, but only so the VA can *save face*. A line in the poem that perfectly reflects the contrast between blacks and whites is *for Negroes only. Under white control*. In that one line the reader runs head-on into the reality that black Americans—and not only the returning veterans—faced. Another line that speaks volumes of discrimination is *ordering colored maids around, white shoes/tapping impatiently.* Another example of how Nelson contrasts black and white.

The larger contrast is between the cowardice and racism of the KKK and the courage of the black doctors and Carver to remain strong in their resolve to support black doctors who arrived to practice medicine at the hospital. Even when he is threatened with death in an anonymous letter, Carver stands firm. Carver himself offers the strongest contrast when he responds to the threat with prayers *for his friend in the Klan.*

Noticing Images

As mentioned above, there is a contrast between black and white in this poem, providing Nelson the opportunity for stark visual images, particularly in this section at the end of the first stanza:

> (White nurses, who were legally excused
> from touching blacks, stood holding their elbows
> and ordering colored maids around, white shoes
> tapping impatiently.)

She juxtaposes white nurses being excused from touching the black patients with these same white nurses ordering around *colored maids*. This is a striking visual image, but Nelson punctuates it with the *sound* of *white shoes/tapping impatiently*.

Noticing Figurative Language

A metaphor is a direct comparison between two seemingly dissimilar things. Poets use metaphors to make an image clear. For a metaphor to be successful and poetic it needs to be more than a cliché—a phrase that is overused in speech or writing. For example, we often say about a strong person, "She's a rock." This comparison gives an image, but the phrase itself is not very original. Look what Nelson does when she says, *the KKK uncoiled/its length and hissed*. She need not say any more or go into more detail about the snake. We get the picture. Indeed, we can *feel* the danger she is describing. With that one metaphor, all seven words of it, she captures the deadly poison of the KKK and their actions.

Noticing Structure

There are a number of turns in the narrative arc of this poem. The first turn in the action occurs between the first and second stanzas. In the first stanza we see the discrimination that the black veterans must endure. With the indented transition to stanza 2—*The Professor joined/the protest*—the poem turns from one of humiliation to one of hope and resistance. Then the KKK counters with its own resistance: "*If you want to stay alive/be away Tuesday.*" Another, and final, turn in the action: *The Professor stayed. And he prayed for his friend in the Klan*. The finality of that last sentence is a fitting conclusion to the poem. As one poet put it, the end of a poem should sound like a door clicking shut. Marilyn Nelson uses this simple but powerful sentence to bring her narrative to a close.

Noticing Repetition

I already mentioned the contrasts in the poem, but those contrasts are emphasized by the repetition of certain words. For example, Nelson uses some form of *veterans* in each of the first three lines, emphasizing that these soldiers fought for their country in World War I, making the treatment they received from the government that much more shameful.

Other words repeated several times are *black* and *white*. The repetition of these words calls attention to the difference between the way people of these races are treated. I will say more about it below, but this particular repetition comes across loud and clear when the poem is read aloud.

AFTER READING: KNOWING THE POEM FOREVER

Say It Out Loud

I think when you read this poem aloud, the key to a good presentation is a change in vocal tone from the first stanza to the second. The voice in the first stanza might be angry at the injustices. Or perhaps resigned to them. But it seems that the voice in the second stanza is more defiant, more confident, as the protest begins and things begin to change. Can you see any other clues to an effective reading of this poem?

You could create a slide show of downloaded historical photographs to use as a backdrop for reading the poem. Research the civil rights movement and find newspaper and news magazine photographs of the era depicting memorable scenes in the movement.

Write About It

Have students explore one of these ideas in their writer's notebook:

1. If you were going to write to George Washington Carver or to his "friend in the Klan," what would you say? Make a list of questions you would ask each person. Or write one of them a letter.

2. The George Washington Carver of the poem is a man of courage who stands up for African Americans. Although most of us don't get the chance to take a stand as important as the one described in "Friends in the Klan," we all experience times when we need to do the right thing. Write about a time when you stood up for something you believed in. Maybe you heard a student making fun of another student. Or your friends tried to get you to do something you knew wasn't right. Or you told the truth even though there were unpleasant consequences.

Issues/Themes/Topics for Discussion

- Racism
- Tolerance
- KKK

142

- Civil rights movement
- African Americans in U.S. military

Related Poems

Harper Audio offers two excellent programs of Langston Hughes reading his poetry: *Essential Langston Hughes Unabridged CD* and *Langston Hughes Reads*. www.harpercollins.com/search/index.aspx?kw=langston%20hughes

If you visit the Academy of American Poets website—www.poets.org—you can find audio clips of Gwendolyn Brooks, Langston Hughes, and Robert Hayden reading their poems.

Another excellent source of audio poetry of African American poets is *I, Too, Sing America: Three Centuries of African American Poetry* (five CDs), which includes, among others, the work of W. E. B. Du Bois, Maya Angelou, Rita Dove, Gwendolyn Brooks, and Amiri Baraka.

Book Bridges

Fiction:

Night Fires, by George Edward Stanley. Thirteen-year-old Woodrow Harper and his mother move to Oklahoma in 1922, and the boy must decide if he can stand up to the Klan.

A Friendship for Today, by Patricia McKissack. A blend of fact and fiction in the semiautobiographical story of Rosemary Patterson and the impact on her life of the landmark *Brown vs. Board of Education* decision.

Lizzie Bright and the Buckminster Boy, by Gary D. Schmidt. An evocative novel based on the sad and shameful actual destruction of a Maine island community in 1912.

Nonfiction:

1963 Birmingham Church Bombing: The Ku Klux Klan's History of Terror, by Lisa Klobuchar. Gives the details of how a Sunday morning bombing in 1963 gave momentum to the civil rights movement.

The Groundbreaking, Chance-Taking Life of George Washington Carver and Science and Invention in America, written and illustrated by Cheryl Harness. Chronicles Carver's rise from slavery to a man whose innovations profoundly changed American farming.

The Story of Ruby Bridges, by Robert Coles. The inspiring true story of an extraordinary six-year-old who helped shape history when she became the first African American sent to first grade in an all-white school.

Online Resources

- One place to get information about the Ku Klux Klan is their website: www.kkk.com. There you'll find links to sites that offer, among other things, information on home schooling, opinions of the Premier Spokeswoman for the White Nationalist Cause, and provocative notions like how "the cross-lighting ceremony is another example of how the national media distorts the Klan image."

- The site of the Southern Poverty Law Center—www.splcenter.org—offers an online magazine, *Teaching Tolerance*, as well as information on hate crimes, the Civil Rights Memorial, and the militia movement.

- The Tuskegee University site—www.tuskegee.edu/Global/category.asp?C =56172&nav=menu200_2—includes a history of the university, which was founded by Dr. Booker T. Washington in 1881. In addition, you can read in-depth information about the legacy of George Washington Carver and the famous Tuskegee Airmen of World War II, the first black aviators.

Name _____ Date _____ Class _____

What Is Courage?

- What is courage?
- Must it be physical?
- Who are two people (people you know, fictional characters, people from the news) who have courage?
- Why do you think these people are courageous?
- What qualities do these people show?

Person	Courageous Qualities
Person	**Courageous Qualities**

Spring Storm

Jim Wayne Miller

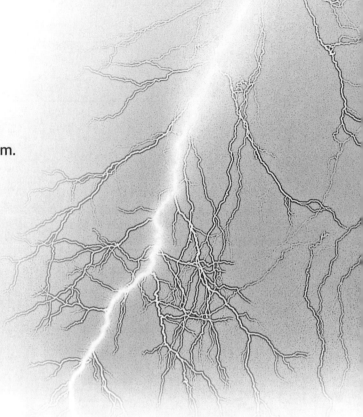

He comes gusting out of the house,
the screen door a thunderclap behind him.

He moves like a black cloud
over the lawn and—stops.

A hand in his mind grabs
a purple crayon of anger
and messes the clean sky.

He sits on the steps, his eye drawing
a mustache on the face in the tree.

As his weather clears,
his rage dripping away,

wisecracks and wonderment
spring up like dandelions.

146

Notes ▶
Observations ▶
Questions ▶

▶ SPRING STORM

Jim Wayne Miller

■ BEFORE READING

Why I Admire This Poem

As I've mentioned before, one of the things I hope for in a poem is surprise. And "Spring Storm" offers a nice surprise in the disconnect between the title and the poem itself. After reading the title, I expected a poem about, well, about a spring storm, a meteorological event. But Miller serves up a storm of a different kind, an emotional storm that the young male character in the poem experiences. The disconnect is similar to what I found in "Friends in the Klan." And, as with the Nelson poem, I was pleasantly surprised by it.

Of course, a good poem must hold more than the surprise of a parlor trick, and Miller skillfully plays out his metaphor of a fast-moving but volatile storm with language choices that create a poignant image. Beyond that, he does what many of the other poets in this book do: focuses on a limited scene or event and carefully builds a poem with details that appeal to the senses.

Companion Poems

In addition to reading this poem with "Friends in the Klan" and discussing the surprise that comes from the disconnect between title and content, you can discuss "Spring Storm" with "Deserted Farm," by Mark Vinz. The subjects of the poems are different, but the poems are similar in their use of extended metaphor.

Special Words to Work Through

Miller's language is simple, and I will discuss it in detail later. However, he gives a different use to a word that we normally use as a noun or an adjective: *gusting*. We usually hear about a *gust of wind* or that *winds were gusty*. But Miller uses it as a verb to describe the action of a person—another example of the kind of surprise I like in a poem.

■ FIRST READING: MEETING THE POEM

Since this poem is about anger, why not ask your students to talk about anger they have experienced. You might use these questions to guide your discussion:

- Can you remember a time you were really angry?

- What were the circumstances?

THEMES, ISSUES, CONCEPTS

- surprise in poetry
- word choice
- anger
- "negative" emotions

LITERARY TERMS

- structure
- narrative
- metaphor

ORGANIZERS

- Narrative

147

- Who was involved?

- How did you react or deal with the anger?

- Did somebody help you deal with it?

- Did you do anything because of your anger that you regretted, that got you into trouble?

The anger captured in this poem quickly and harmlessly dissipates, as the boy reverts to *wisecracks and wonderment*. Not all bouts of anger end so quickly or so benignly, of course.

The emotion at the heart of this poem is a so-called "negative emotion," like apathy, grief, fear, hatred, shame, regret, resentment, anger, and hostility. Nevertheless, we and our students have all experienced such "negative" emotions. The key is how we deal with them. You might consider inviting a school counselor or psychologist to discuss negative emotions and offer suggestions for dealing with them.

CLOSE READING: GETTING TO KNOW THE POEM

Although "Spring Storm" is a straightforward narrative, it does have some metaphorical language that might puzzle some of the literal thinkers in your class. But the figurative language that Miller uses is apt and well done and captures the emotions of the character. As you discuss the metaphorical aspects of the poem, ask your students what figurative language they might have used to express some of their feelings. Have they been "down in the dumps"? Or "on cloud nine"?

Noticing Structure

Distribute copies of "Spring Storm" and give your students time to read through it a couple of times, marking it up and jotting down their observations and questions. No doubt they will recognize the narrative, or story line. Each stanza—most of which are only two lines long—is a step in the narrative arc of the poem, which mirrors a spring rainstorm.

Distribute copies of the **Narrative** organizer and have your students jot down the steps in the narrative along the plot line provided. Ask them to pay particular attention to the high point, or climax, of the story. Once students have filled out the organizer, discuss the events of the poem.

The opening lines in the first two stanzas follow a pattern of depicting an action: *he* followed by a verb:

He comes gusting out of the house
He moves like a black cloud

But the fourth stanza changes the pace of the narrative: *He sits on the steps*. The fifth and sixth stanzas mark the turning point of the poem and the falling action that follows.

Noticing Figurative Language

This poem is built on the central metaphor of a spring storm. Along the way, Miller uses other metaphors and similes that fit in with this central metaphor. Ask your class to underline any reference to a rainstorm. Once they have marked up their poem, you can discuss the figurative language in the poem.

Take a look at the first stanza. In those two lines, we see the angry boy in language related to a storm: *gusting out of the house*, the *thunderclap* of the screen door as it bangs shut. In the next stanza—also just two lines long—we find a simile as part of the description: *He moves like a black cloud*. After five lines in the middle of the poem without references to a storm, Miller is back to the storm metaphor in stanza 5: *As his weather clears, his rage dripping away*. He finishes up with a showers-bring-dandelions simile in the final two-line stanza.

Noticing Word Choice

In addition to the storm words and phrases in this poem, there are a few other spots that are more related to the emotional storm in the boy rather than to a physical storm. In the second stanza, the boy who moved *like a black cloud* suddenly stops on the front lawn. The third and fourth stanzas, while devoid of references to weather, use other metaphors to show the emotional state of the character.

In stanza 3 the boy *messes the clean sky* with his *purple crayon of anger*. Miller shows his character's emotional state in a metaphor that suggests purposely coloring badly in a coloring book. In the next stanza, the boy rests, but his anger is only slightly diminished, *his eye drawing/a moustache on the face in the tree*. More acting out, though still metaphorical (graffiti).

The final two stanzas show the end of the storm, *his anger dripping away*, just as rain does at the end of a storm. The storm has provided the nutrients for *wisecracks and wonderment*, a nicely alliterative phrase, with its repetition of the initial /w/ sound.

149

AFTER READING: **KNOWING THE POEM FOREVER**

Say It Out Loud

As in a rainstorm, there is a lot of energy in this poem, especially in the first few stanzas, so any performance needs to convey the energy that comes from the boy's anger, which seems most intense in the first two stanzas, lessens slightly in stanzas 3 and 4, then dissipates in the last two stanzas. A performance must reflect that change in energy. There is only one character in "Spring Storm," so you might want to have someone pantomime the actions of the boy while someone else reads the words. The actor must be able to convey emotions with actions, but also with facial expressions, from *gusting out of the house* to the *wisecracks and merriment*.

Write About It

Have students explore one of these ideas in their writer's notebook:

1. Write a personal narrative about a time you were angry. Here are some questions to get you started (you may have already discussed some of these):

    - Can you remember a time you were really angry?
    - What were the circumstances?
    - Who was involved?
    - How did you react or deal with the anger?
    - Did somebody help you deal with it?
    - Did you do anything that you regretted, that got you into trouble?

    These questions are only guidelines. You may already know exactly what you want to write about.

2. What do you think happened in the home before the boy *stormed* out the door? Write a dialogue between him and another character or two in the house (his parents, for example). What did they argue about? Who said what to whom leading up to his angry exit? Create the other characters as well as the things they said to one another. Your dialogue will look like a play. Don't forget to add stage directions, so your actors will know what to do in addition to what to say.

3. If you were going to make a short film of this poem, what would be the main parts of the narrative? Try to "translate" this poem into a storyboard of your film. In other words, draw each of the scenes that helps this narrative unfold. You could caption each scene with the appropriate line(s) from the poem.

Issues/Themes/Topics for Discussion

- Anger
- "Negative" emotions
- Coping with emotions

Related Poems

Here are a few poems that deal with "negative" emotions:

"Lonesome," by Myra Cohn Livingston

"My Stupid Parakeet Named After You," by X. J. Kennedy

"Teased," by Richard J. Margolis

"Blubber Lips," by Jim Daniels

"If I Could Put a Curse on You," by Paul B. Janeczko

Book Bridges

How to Take the Grrrr Out of Anger by Elizabeth Verdick and Marjorie Lisovskis. Young readers will find lots of advice and suggestions in this book about issues like how to recognize anger and how to deal with anger in others, including "6 Steps to Solving Anger Problems."

Racing the Past by Sis Deans. Eleven-year-old Ricky's abusive father is dead, and the boy needs to help his younger brother deal with lingering fear of the man, while handling his own anger and the teasing of some schoolyard bullies.

The Janitor's Boy by Andrew Clements. It's not easy for Jack when his fifth-grade classmates tease him because his father is the janitor at their school. Jack turns his anger onto his father.

Online Resources

- The University of Virginia has a good site about bullying in middle school: youthviolence.edschool.virginia.edu/bullying/bullying-middle-school-research.html. The site offers some sobering statistics as well as a number of helpful links to bullying prevention programs.

- The January 2006 issue of *Middle School Journal*—a publication of the National Middle School Association—includes a thoughtful article, "Bullying in Middle Schools: Prevention and Intervention." You can find the article here: www.nmsa.org/Publications/MiddleSchoolJournal/Articles/January2006/Article2/tabid/693/Default.aspx.

- You can read "Anger Management and Schools" in a publication of the University of North Florida—www.unf.edu/dept/fie/sdfs/notes/anger.pdf—to find out how some schools are dealing with anger management issues.

Narrative in "Spring Storm"

Jot down the various stages of the story in "Spring Storm," including the climax of the story and the falling action at the end of the poem.

© 2011 by Paul B. Janeczko from *Reading Poetry in the Middle Grades*. Portsmouth, NH: Heinemann.

Foul Shot

Edwin A. Hoey

Notes ▶
Observations ▶
Questions ▶

With two 60s stuck on the scoreboard
And two seconds hanging on the clock,
The solemn boy in the center of eyes,
Squeezed by silence,
Seeks out the line with his feet,
Soothes his hands along his uniform,
Gently drums the ball against the floor,
Then measures the waiting net,
Raises the ball on his right hand,
Balances it with his left,
Calms it with fingertips,
Breathes,
Crouches,
Waits,
And then through a stretching of stillness,
Nudges it upward.

The ball
Slides up and out,
Lands,
Leans,
Wobbles,
Wavers,
Hesitates,
Plays it coy
Until every face begs with unsounding screams—
And then
        And then
                And then,

Right before ROAR-UP,
Dives down and through.

154

▶ FOUL SHOT

Edwin A. Hoey

BEFORE READING

Why I Admire This Poem

I'm not much of a basketball fan, but I am a big fan of giving kids poetry that will excite them about the genre and open them to the possibility that, yes, poems *can* be about things like sports. "Foul Shot" will connect with any of your students who are familiar with the pressure of an athletic event. Some may fantasize about being *the solemn boy* at the foul line with the game on the line. Others may equate the pressure in a basketball game with a nonathletic pressure they have experienced. And let's not forget the fans. They, too, feel the tension in a situation like the one in "Foul Shot." The reason so many of us react to this poem is because Hoey does a great job of conveying the excitement and tension of a tied basketball game with *two seconds on the clock.*

"Foul Shot" is also an excellent model for kids' own writing, especially kids who may not have had much exposure to poems about sports.

Companion Poems

Because one of the strongest elements in "Foul Shot" is the tension Hoey creates, compare the tension in this poem with the tension in these poems:

"Speak Up," by Janet S. Wong

"Hoods," by Paul B. Janeczko

"Friends in the Klan," by Marilyn Nelson

Special Words to Work Through

I'll have more to say later about the way Hoey sees language in this poem, because his word choice is one of its strengths. For now, here are a few words your students may not know: *solemn, wobbles, wavers, nudges,* and *coy.*

FIRST READING: MEETING THE POEM

Ask your students to share moments of pressure they have experienced. Was it during a game? A penalty kick in soccer? The bottom of the last inning with a winning run at third? The first day at a new school? A solo in a band concert or religious service? What was at stake at those moments? Was the pressure imposed on them, say,

THEMES, ISSUES, CONCEPTS

- tension in poetry
- performing under pressure
- active verbs
- fame

LITERARY TERMS

- alliteration
- repetition
- structure
- personification
- line breaks

ORGANIZERS

- Active Verbs
- Plot

155

by a parent or a coach? Or was some of it self-inflicted? In other words, did they bring some of the pressure on themselves, maybe by bragging that they would come through when it mattered most? Did they ask the coach to put them in a game? Ask the band director to trust them with a solo? Some people feel they work better under pressure. Do you or your students feel that way? Ask your students what happened next. Did they rise to the occasion and succeed? Did they fail miserably? In either case, did the pressure factor into the results?

Once you've heard some of your students' tales of performing under pressure, read aloud "Foul Shot," stopping before the final two lines. Leave the outcome a mystery. Take a survey—how many of your students think the foul shot dropped through the net? Are there any clues in the poem to prepare the reader for the success or failure of the shot? Then hand out copies of the poem so students can read it themselves and find out what happened.

CLOSE READING: GETTING TO KNOW THE POEM

One of the things I like to tell young writers, regardless of age, is that writing a poem is a lot like writing a report on a science experiment, at least as far as the *process* is concerned. Both the poet and scientist follow the same basic procedures: observe and report.

The scientist performs an experiment, observes the results, gathers data, considers that data, and writes a report (in prose) laced with graphs and charts. The poet goes through much the same process. She observes what is going on around her out there in the world but also what is going on *inside* her. She then writes her report, a poem, using the absolute best words to do so.

Hoey observes and reports on two seconds of a lifetime, two seconds when the game is on the line—an incredibly small part of a person's life, but, at that moment, it *is* that person's life, not to the mention the lives of the fans. Hoey does it all through close (microscopic?) observation and exquisite word choice.

Noticing Active Verbs

A major element of a good poem is the detail the poet uses to create an image that appeals to one or more of our senses. Hoey uses active and descriptive verbs, more so than adjectives, to create the central image in "Foul Shot."

Look at the sequence of action early in the poem: *squeezed, seeks out, soothes, drums, measures.* And there are others. Distribute copies of the **Active Verbs** organizer, which asks your students to list the verbs in the poem as well as the objects of those verbs (for example, *drums | the ball*). Students might feel more comfortable completing this activity in small groups. Write the students' lists of verbs and objects on the board. What can they say about this long list of verbs and objects? How about the way Hoey piles up these phrases, building tension in the poem, as one action quickly follows another?

Alliteration

Remind your students that alliteration is the repetition of initial consonant sounds. They need look no further than the first six lines of this poem to find ample examples of this poetic technique, in this case the repetition of the /s/ sound.

Divide the class into groups of two or three students. Tell them to be on the lookout for examples of alliteration in the poem. Ask them to follow along in the poem as you read it aloud. I would even read it twice. Since alliteration is about sound, students need the chance to *hear* the poem. When your students have written down examples of alliteration in the poem, ask them to share these examples with the class as you highlight them on a projected transparency of the poem.

Here are a few examples (beyond the first six lines) they should have noticed: *lands/leans, wobbles/wavers, right/roar.* Are there others?

Noticing Repetition

Like most free verse poems, this one has no set rhythm, nothing like that in "The Wreck of the *Hesperus*," for example. Nonetheless "Foul Shot" does contain neat little patches of rhythm. Can your students hear the rhythm of these lines, which mostly relies on the verb/object arrangement we've already discussed?

Soothes his hands along his uniform,
Gently drums the ball against the floor,
Then measures the waiting net,
Raises the ball on his right hand,
Balances it with his left,
Calms it with fingertips

And look at these lines in the second stanza:

Lands,
Leans,
Wobbles,
Wavers,
Hesitates,
Plays it coy

In addition to the /l/ and /w/ alliteration, notice how the *l* words contain a single syllable, the *w*-words contain two syllables, and the next two lines each contain three syllables. Increasing the syllables in these lines adds to the tension of the moment as the ball hovers on the rim of the basket.

Since poetry is about sound—among other things—any discussion of a poem's rhythm must take place in the context of out-loud readings. Don't be afraid to read sections of the poem a couple of times or, better, have students read them. Let the class *hear* the rhythm of the poem.

Noticing Stanza Structure

Hoey divides his poem into three stanzas, each advancing the plot of the poem. Distribute the **Plot** organizer and have students read each stanza of the poem—they are printed in the column on the left—and explain in the space to the right how that stanza advances the plot.

The first stanza sets the scene: tie score in a basketball game with two seconds left to play, and the *solemn boy* stepping up to the free-throw line, needing to sink one basket to win the game. This stanza ends when the boy *nudges* the basketball *upward*. The second stanza traces the path of the ball, from his hands to the rim. The final two-line stanza documents the boy's success.

Noticing Line Breaks

As you've worked through the poems in this book, your students have had many chances to talk about line breaks. They can bring all this experience to bear in talking about the line breaks in this poem. However, one thing is especially noteworthy: nearly every line ends with a comma. What does that mean to the poem? Hoey is forcing us to pause at the end of those lines—not stop, just pause. Those pauses help build tension by giving the reader a touch of the silence that squeezes the boy as he stands on the free-throw line. Read the poem aloud without the commas, taking only the almost imperceptible pauses we use at the end of lines of free verse without punctuation. Then read it the way Hoey wrote it, pausing at the commas. Can you hear the difference? Those pauses make the poem far more suspenseful.

Noticing Personification

Hoey doesn't use much figurative language in "Foul Shot." It's worthwhile to point out to your students that this is a successful poem that doesn't need figurative language. Hoey brings the scene to life with his overall word choice, active verbs, and line breaks. Nonetheless, he does personify the ball in a couple of instances. In line 11 he writes that the boy *calms it with fingertips*, and in line 24, the ball *plays it coy*. What scant figurative language Hoey uses, he uses well.

AFTER READING: KNOWING THE POEM FOREVER

Say It Out Loud

This poem offers some interesting performance possibilities. One is to read it in the voice of a game announcer, initially getting caught up in the silence as the boy lines up his shot, then growing more excited as the *the ball/slides up and out*, until the final outburst of the *ROAR-UP* at the end of the poem.

Another possibility is to divide the poem into small parts, each one spoken by a fan in the stands. In fact, a small bleacher/folding chair section of fans is a good visual, as various fans speak a line or two, perhaps leaning in to the person next to him or her. The performance ends with all the fans rising and shouting out the final two lines.

Write About It

Have students explore one of these ideas in their writer's notebook:

1. Rewrite the poem as an article for the local or school newspaper. Keep the basic details, but add some color by describing things like the importance of the game, perhaps between arch rivals or for the conference championship. Because the poem describes only two seconds of the game, you'll need to add information about the game leading up to that final shot. And don't forget to describe the mayhem in the celebration following the game.

2. Imagine what the boy would say about the game. Is he the star of the team who just did what others expected of him? Or is he a marginal player who was thrust into his moment of glory? What was going through his mind as he approached the final seconds of the game? Write the text message or email he sends to a friend who wasn't there. Add details that make sense.

Issues/Themes/Topics for Discussion

- Performing under pressure
- The importance of team sports

Related Poems

"Nothing But Net," by Roy Scheele

"The Hummer," by William Matthews

"Shooting," by B. H. Fairchild

"Pitcher," by Robert Francis

"Ex-Basketball Player," by John Updike

159

Book Bridges

Fiction:

Jump Shot, a novel-in-verse by Mel Glenn, which mixes first-person voices of players, fans, and newspaper articles. Be advised that there is a fatal bus accident at the end of the novel.

Roughnecks by Thomas Cochran follows Travis, who cost his high school football team an undefeated season, as he looks for his chance for redemption.

Spelldown by Karon Luddy. Thirteen-year-old Karlene Bridges studies her family's two-volume dictionary as she tries to deal with her father's alcoholism. Only when her Latin teacher begins to coach her, does Karlene's confidence soar.

Travel Team by Mike Lupica. After his cut from his travel basketball team, twelve-year-old Danny Walker organizes his own team of other kids who were cut from the team. Does this team have a shot at victory?

Rimshots: Basketball Pix, Rolls, and Rhythms by Charles R. Smith, Jr., serves up an exciting collection of stories and poems about playing basketball.

Nonfiction:

Slam Dunk!: Science Projects with Basketball by Robert Gardner and Dennis Shortelle. Learn about friction, mass, vectors, and more in this book of basketball-related experiments. In addition, great science project ideas follow many experiments.

Basketball by Mark Stewart. A book of those moments in basketball history where one great short or defensive move is often the difference between winning and loosing.

Online Resources

Where can you go to find things basketball? Lots of places! Among the best are:

- You can find the best of the best at the NBA hall of fame site, The Naismith Memorial Basketball Hall of Fame: www.hoophall.com.

- For information about the history of basketball, you can look here: www.sportsknowhow.com/basketball/history/basketball-history.shtml

- If you're more interested in finding out about college basketball, you can start at the NCAA site: www.ncaa.org.

Name _____ Date _____ Class _____

Active Verbs in "Foul Shot"

Verbs	Objects
1. Seeks out	the line

Plot in "Foul Shot"

"Foul Shot"	How Stanza Advances Plot
With two 60's stuck on the scoreboard And two seconds hanging on the clock, The solemn boy in the center of eyes, Squeezed by silence, Seeks out the line with his feet, Soothes his hands along his uniform, Gently drums the ball against the floor, Then measures the waiting net, Raises the ball on his right hand, Balances it with his left, Calms it with fingertips, Breathes, Crouches, Waits, And then through a stretching of stillness, Nudges it upward.	

The ball
Slides up and out,
Lands,
Leans,
Wobbles,
Wavers,
Hesitates,
Plays it coy
Until every face begs with unsounding
screams—
And then
       And then
             And then,	

Right before ROAR-UP, Dives down and through.	

A Hot Property

Ronald Wallace

I am not. I am
an also-ran,
a bridesmaid, a finalist,
a second-best bed. I am
the one they could just
as easily have given it to
but didn't.
I'm the one who was just
edged, shaded, bested, nosed out.
I made the final cut,
the short list,
the long deliberation.
I'm good, very good,
but I'm not good enough.
I'm an alternate, a backup,
a very close decision,
a red ribbon, a handshake,
a glowing commendation.
You don't know me.
I've a dozen names,
all honorably mentioned.
I could be anybody.

Notes ▶
Observations ▶
Questions ▶

From *Reading Poetry in the Middle Grades.* Portsmouth, NH: Heinemann. © 1983 by the University of Pittsburgh Press from *Tunes for Bears to Dance To* by Ronald Wallace. Reprinted by permission of the University of Pittsburgh Press.

164

Roland Wallace

BEFORE READING

Why I Admire This Poem

Here is another poem in which surprise adds a wonderful spark. Surprise often lurks in the narrative arc or the ending, but can also be delivered by the poet's choice of language or her take on a subject or a situation. I like a poet who can do what Emily Dickinson describes when she says, "Tell all the Truth but tell it slant." Telling it slant is often surprising.

The surprise in this Ronald Wallace poem begins with the title. "A Hot Property" leads us to believe the poem is about, well, a hot property. Something sought after and valuable. But Wallace's title runs on into the first line of the poem. The opening of the poem is really, *A Hot Property/I am not.* Ah, now we have a better idea of what the poem is *really* about, a narrator who feels he is, in many ways, what he says mid-poem: *I'm good,/but not good enough.*

Companion Poems

Since "A Hot Property" is a list poem, you could use it in connection with "Every Cat Has a Story," by Naomi Shihab Nye. It addresses an issue almost all young people confront at some point, so it can be linked thematically with "Spring Storm," by Jim Wayne Miller.

Special Words to Work Through

This poem is based on expressions that convey not being "good enough." Your students will know phrases like *second-best* and *honorable mention.* However, they might not know that a *finalist* is a person whose work makes all the cuts in a competition, including the *final cut,* but ends up not being the winner. (And though it may be an honor just to be nominated, it's not the same as winning, not by a long shot.)

Distribute copies of the poem to your students. Ask them to read it and underline all the words and phrases that mean "not good enough." After five minutes or so, ask what they found and highlight their responses—in a bright color, if you can—on a transparency of the poem. (If they miss any of the phrases, highlight those as well.)

Next, hand out copies of the **Expressions** organizer and ask them to think about the expressions Wallace uses in the poem and what they mean—for example, a red ribbon is inferior to the traditional blue ribbon given for first place. Then ask what

THEMES, ISSUES, CONCEPTS

- popularity
- who am I?
- surprise in poetry
- feeling left out
- belonging

LITERARY TERMS

- list poem
- repetition
- structure

ORGANIZERS

- Expressions

165

other expressions indicate something is not good enough? What expressions do they use that Wallace doesn't? They may suggest *second fiddle* or *second banana*. Ask them to compare their list with the expressions Wallace uses in his poem. What do they notice about the list? Is theirs harsher than Wallace's? Are their expressions more visual?

FIRST READING: MEETING THE POEM

Ask your students to think of a time when they felt inferior, "not good enough." It could be when they were compared with a friend or somebody in their family or it could be related to a sports competition. A boy might have an older brother who always puts him down. A girl might feel inferior when she compares herself with fashion models in magazine ads. What stories do they feel comfortable sharing? Do their stories include any of the expressions they listed after reading the Wallace poem? Can you add a story of your own?

After they have had a chance to tell their stories, ask them to describe in a few words how they *felt* at the time. What sorts of words do they use? Do any of them use comparisons?

CLOSE READING: GETTING TO KNOW THE POEM

"A Hot Property" is a list poem. Remind your class that a list poem is not merely a random list of things that are related to a topic. A good list poem has structure, organization, and rich language. Wallace chooses the phrases in the poem carefully to create the overall feeling the narrator has of being *edged, shaded, bested, nosed out*—in other words, second best. He matches the content of the poem with its form.

Noticing Repetition

Repetition of the word *I* is one of the things that holds this poem together. It's used ten times in the twenty-two-line poem:

- *I am* or *I'm* appears seven times.
- *I* followed by a verb appears two times
- *I've* appears once.

But this repeated pronoun is always used at the start of a sentence (or in one instance, a clause), which makes it even more noticeable. This is what I call an I-poem, a poem in which a poet explores his identity, his place in the world.

Noticing Structure

Your students will readily see that "A Hot Property" is free verse. Even though there is no predicable rhythm or rhyme, Wallace does a few things to make sure the poem holds together. While the poem is a single stanza, it is divided into five sections, each one beginning with *I*. Each section uses a new list of expressions for not being "good enough."

I always pay a little extra attention to the beginning and ending of a poem. Does the beginning draw you in? When you reach the end, do you have a sense that the poem is finished? In this case, Wallace uses the title as part of the first line to hook us: *A Hot Property/I am not*. He turns the tables on us, then works his way through the poem, showing us all the ways the narrator is "not good enough." The last three lines then bring the poem to a satisfying conclusion:

> I've a dozen names,
> all honorably mentioned.
> I could be anybody.

With these three lines we get to the larger truth of the poem. All the while the narrator has been talking about his own experiences and feelings, he really is speaking for all of us who have felt "not good enough" from time to time.

I like the ambiguity of *I could be anybody*. It can be taken literally, in that nearly everybody feels not good enough at one time or another. But there is also nothing noteworthy about the narrator. By saying, *I could be anybody*, he is saying, "I'm nobody."

AFTER READING: KNOWING THE POEM FOREVER

Say It Out Loud

Although this poem has a single narrator, a key to performing it lies in the line, *I've a dozen names*. Since the narrator could be anyone/everyone in the class, everyone in the class can take part. Some students can read whole sentences and phrases, like *I am/an also-ran* or *I made the final cut*. Other lines can be broken into two- or three-word phrases, each read by a different person. For example:

> I am
> an alternate,
> a backup
> a very close decision,
> a red ribbon,
> a handshake,
> a glowing commendation

Write About It

Have students explore one of these ideas in their writer's notebook:

1. This poem is about not feeling "good enough." Have you ever felt that way? Write about it. What were the circumstances? Did someone say something to you or do something to you to leave you feeling not good enough? Was it a feeling that you were able to get over? Do your best to include details. You might turn what happened into a short play, with a setting and dialogue.

2. While the poem is told from the point of view of a narrator who has taken a hit to his self-esteem, there's also the other side of that issue: the times you do or say things that damage someone else's self-esteem. Perhaps it's an unkind word or an act of exclusion. Deliberate or not, the effect on the other person is often the same. Try writing a letter to that person apologizing or explaining your actions.

3. Take another look at how Wallace builds "A Hot Property." Then write a list poem with a narrator who really *is* a hot property. What phrases would you include to show that? Remember, your poem shouldn't be merely a list of phrases. Your first draft might start out that way, but through thoughtful revision you have the opportunity to look at the language you use, as well as the overall structure and organization.

Issues/Themes/Topics for Discussion

- Feeling left out
- Feeling not good enough
- Excluding others
- Including others
- Belonging

Related Poems

"Rites of Passage," by Dorianne Laux

"The Telling Tree," by Linda Peavy

"Camp Calvary," by Ronald Wallace

"Fifteen," by William Stafford

"Ronnie Schwinck," by David Allan Evans

Book Bridges

Tangerine by Edward Bloor. Paul, who is legally blind, dreams of playing soccer. But can he make the team at Tangerine Middle School, where the soccer team is one of toughest group of kids at the school.

Queen of Second Place by Laura Peyton Roberts. The good-but-not-good enough girl Cassie Howard sets her sights on one of the coolest kids at Hilltop High. How far will Cassie go to nab the guy and get the best of her rival?

Notes From a Liar and Her Dog by Gennifer Choldenko. Lying has become a way of life for Antonia, but can she change her ways when a new teacher takes her under her wing? Can Ant stop lying?

Online Resources

- Because this poem is based on euphemisms, those mild or indirect expressions used in place of blunt or harsh words, you might want to take a look at www.euphemismlist.com, a site that gives a long list of euphemisms and their explanations.

- You can find a lesson for teaching euphemisms to ESL students at www.yourdictionary.com/esl/Euphemism-Lessons.html. Actually, this is a good lesson to introduce younger students to this aspect of our language.

Name _____ Date _____ Class _____

Expressions in "A Hot Property"

Expression	Explanation

JUNKYARDS

Julian Lee Rayford

You take any junkyard
   and you will see it filled with
   symbols of progress
   remarkable things discarded

What civilization went ahead on
   all its onward-impelling implements
   are given over to the junkyards
   to rust

The supreme implement, the wheel
   is conspicuous in the junkyards

The axles and the levers
   the cogs and the flywheels
   all the parts of dynamos
   all the parts of motors
   fall the parts of rusting.

172

Notes ▶
Observations ▶
Questions ▶

From *Reading Poetry in the Middle Grades*. Portsmouth, NH: Heinemann. © 1981 by David Ray from *From A to Z: 200 Contemporary American Poets*, published by Swallow Press. Reprinted by permission of David Ray.

Julian Lee Rayford

BEFORE

Why I Admire This Poem

I frequently think of progress and technological advances in terms of my writing career. The first book I published I wrote on a typewriter—a red IBM Selectric that hummed and clattered—and I was halfway through the handwritten draft of my second book when my Apple computer arrived. That machine—an Apple IIe with a large floppy-disk drive—changed my life as a writer.

Then came the Internet. In ways too numerous to count, it has made my life easier and better. I can communicate more easily with friends and family. All of my manuscripts are submitted electronically. Arranging and making author visits and appearances—booking flights and motels, ironing out details with a sponsoring school, being able to keep up to date with my emails (and baseball scores) while I'm away from home—is easier than it ever was. Yet, as we know, "progress" is a double-edged sword, and I'm not sure that students see both sides. I included this poem to get the students thinking about the world around them. They will be inheriting the care of the world before they know it, maybe before they are ready for it. Perhaps a poem like "Junkyards" will get them thinking about that day.

Companion Poems

You might want to discuss "Junkyards" in connection with "Abandoned Farmhouse" and "Deserted Farm," which deal with the natural reclamation of land that was once inhabited, a "progress" of sorts.

Special Words to Work Through

This poem contains some challenging words for your students: *discarded, onward-impelling, implement, conspicuous.* In addition, there are words that name earlier examples of tools: *axles, levers, cogs, flywheels, dynamos.*

Before discussing any of these words with your students, it's important that they know what a junkyard is. They may think of it as a landfill, where junk is dumped, but that's not true. Some people call a junkyard a "salvage yard," and I find that to be a more apt designation because it is a place where you can go to buy used parts for your car or truck. You can recycle usable parts that people have discarded, and save some money in the deal.

THEMES, ISSUES, CONCEPTS

- What is "progress"?
- recycling
- life cycles
- archeology of junk

LITERARY TERMS

- structure
- lament

ORGANIZERS

- Progress
- Time Capsule

173

I suggest a minilesson/research project on the tools and implements that are mentioned in the poem, so students can understand not only what they are but also why they were included in a poem about "progress." Here are a couple of sites where your class can find information on levers:

- www.enchantedlearning.com/physics/machines/Levers.shtml
- www.fi.edu/pieces/knox/automaton/lever.htm

A little research on axles will show your students how this simple "tool"—a component of all vehicles, from trucks to trains—helps move the world. You might ask a science or physics teacher in your high school to visit your class and talk about these simple tools.

FIRST READING: MEETING THE POEM

The notion of "progress" offers an opportunity for a lively class discussion. What *is* progress? What do your students think of when they hear that word? Does it have a good connotation? A bad connotation? Can they name examples of positive progress that resulted in unanticipated negative consequences? (The pollution that came with the automobile is one example.)

Which technological advance has most impacted their lives? For some students it might be the computer. Others might list the MP3 player or the cell phone. What negative or unanticipated consequences have these advances brought with them? Some of your students—most of them?—might see no negative consequences of the cell phone, for example. Remind them to consider what other people, like their parents, might find a negative impact of cell phones. Ah, the discussion should be rich.

After the students have had a chance to offer some examples in your discussion, break the class into groups of two or three students. Give each student a copy of the **Progress** organizer. Have each group think about technological changes that they know from history or that they have experienced in their lives. For three such advances, ask them to list the benefits of that bit of "progress," then list any unanticipated consequences of that advance.

CLOSE READING: GETTING TO KNOW THE POEM

"Junkyards" seems almost a lament. There's a sadness about junkyards *filled/with symbols of progress*, where *fall the parts of rusting*. It's also a poem about impermanence. Even the *supreme implement, the wheel/is conspicuous in the junkyards*. In fact, all of these basic tools, like axles and levers, these implements that *civilization went ahead on*, lie rusting in the junkyard.

After the class has had time to talk about impermanence and the ever-changing world, give your students a copy of the **Time Capsule** organizer. In the left column, they are to write four or five items that are important parts of the current American or world culture. Remind them that their time capsule will be dug up in twenty-five or fifty years, so their items must be things that clearly are important to people in our culture. They could include an object, like a cell phone, or technologies, like Facebook. In the other column they should write their reasons for including that item or technology. Assume that the capsule is size of a large suitcase (or something larger, if you wish).

Noticing Structure

Give a copy of "Junkyards" to your students. Ask them to underline what they consider the most important words in the poem. (You might have a transparency version of the poem ready on which to record their responses.) Or, the students might also just call the words out, popcorn style, to get a sense of big ideas. If students repeat words it makes the words/ideas even more prominent. As they share the words they underlined, they'll see that many of them are at the ends of lines, where poets often place their important words.

Your students may also notice that there is no punctuation in the poem. But does it need punctuation? Look at the first stanza:

> You take any junkyard
> and you will see it filled with
> symbols of progress
> remarkable things discarded

Don't we pause slightly after the words *junkyard* and *progress*? Ask a couple of your students to read this stanza aloud. Chances are they will pause oh so slightly at the end of line 1 and line 3, at the key words. Line 2 ends with a preposition, so readers will slide into the next line. What about line 4? Your readers will stop there even though there is no punctuation, because there is a stanza break between that line and the first line of the next stanza. But the firmness of *discarded* is also a logical place to stop; the word hangs in the air, waiting for the next idea.

AFTER READING: KNOWING THE POEM FOREVER

Say It Out Loud

I think this poem needs to be read straightforwardly. But that doesn't mean you can't make it an interesting performance. As far as staging goes, your players might be looking out into the audience, as if they are looking over a fence into a junkyard.

Before you decide how to perform the poem, read it over a number of times and look for places to make logical breaks, places where you might want to switch to a different reader. For example, I think the first stanza could be broken into three parts: line 1, lines 2–3, and line 4. Look over the rest of the poem, dividing it into parts for different readers in ways that will help the audience understand it.

Write About It

Have your students explore one of these ideas in their writer's notebook:

1. What inventions do you envision for the future? Something to help with chores in the home? Maybe a dishwasher that puts the dishes away? What changes do you foresee in the field of communication? Will future generations have a phone implanted in their neck? Working with another student or two, brainstorm some inventions of the future. When you've come up with an interesting list, pick one and create an ad campaign for it. You can prepare a print ad for a magazine, or a brief commercial for radio or television. Let your imagination go!

2. Your class discussed which cultural items it would put into a time capsule. Now suppose you are making a time capsule of items that reflect your *personal* life. Which items will you include? A trendy fashion item? A technological gadget? Write a list of the things you would include, as well as the reason each item made your list. Remember, the things you place in your time capsule must truly reflect you. Assume your time capsule is about the size of a large suitcase.

3. Try writing about something you have either kept that you should have discarded or something you discarded that you wish you had kept? Describe the object. What was your attachment to it? How did you finally come to make your decision about it?

Issues/Themes/Topics for Discussion

- Progress
- Basic tools
- Oxidation
- Recycling
- Your legacy to future generations

Related Poems

J. Patrick Lewis has written a book of nifty science poems called *Scien-trickery: Riddles in Science*. Among my favorites is "It's the Pits," a riddle about rust, which fits in well with "Junkyards."

Other poems about "progress":

"White Trash," by Jim Hall

"Stripped," by George Ella Lyon

"Mining Town," by X. J. Kennedy

Book Bridges

The Junkyard Dog by Erika Tamar. Eleven-year-old Katie decides to feed an abused junkyard dog. She soon realizes that feeding the dog is not enough as the hard winter begins. With the advice of her stepfather, she builds a dog house for the dog.

Seedfolks by Paul Fleischman. A moving story of how a trash-filled lot is transformed through the good will and hard work of neighbors. In the process of transforming a space in the city, the people notice changes in their lives.

What Can We Do About Trash and Recycling? by Lorijo Metz. Part of the Protecting Our Planet series, this book gives young readers basic information about the relationships between trash disposal and pollution.

Online Resources

- Here's an interesting article about a real time capsule and efforts to find it: www.ctvbc.ctv.ca/servlet/an/local/CTVNews/20100107/bc_time_capsule_search_100107/20100107/?hub=BritishColumbiaHome

- This photographic website—photojojo.com/timecapsule/—offers an interesting take on the time capsule. Set up an account and twice a month you will get an email with your photos from the previous year!

- www.timecapsulesinc.com/time-capsule-photos.htm contains pictures of time capsules from a company that manufacturers them. Even if you're not in the market for a time capsule, this site makes fascinating browsing.

Name _____ Date _____ Class _____

Progress

Technological Advances	Benefits	Unanticipated Consequences

Name _____ Date _____ Class _____

Time Capsule _____

What Would You Place in a Time Capsule?	Why Would You Include This Item?

Nothing Gold Can Stay

Robert Frost

Nature's first green is gold,
Her hardest hue to hold,
Her early leaf's a flower;
But only so an hour.

Then leaf subsides to leaf.
So Eden sank to grief,
So dawn goes down to day.
Nothing gold can stay.

180

From *Reading Poetry in the Middle Grades*. Portsmouth, NH: Heinemann. © 1951 by Robert Frost. © 1923, 1969 by Henry Holt and Company from *The Poetry of Robert Frost*, edited by Edward Connery Lathem. Reprinted by permission of Henry Holt and Company, LLC.

Nothing Gold Can Stay

Robert Frost

Nature's first green is gold,
Her hardest hue to hold,
Her early leaf's a flower;
But only so an hour.

Then leaf subsides to leaf.
So Eden sank to grief,
So dawn goes down to day.
Nothing gold can stay.

Notes ▶
Observations ▶
Questions ▶

From *Reading Poetry in the Middle Grades*. Portsmouth, NH: Heinemann. © 1951 by Robert Frost. © 1923, 1969 by Henry Holt and Company from *The Poetry of Robert Frost*, edited by Edward Connery Lathem. Reprinted by permission of Henry Holt and Company, LLC.

Time Capsule _____

What Would You Place in a Time Capsule?	Why Would You Include This Item?

▶ NOTHING GOLD CAN STAY

Robert Frost

BEFORE READING

Why I Admire This Poem

I enjoy sharing this poem with students because it does a lot of things well and therefore is a good model for readers who aren't quite sure what makes a good poem. For one thing, "Nothing Gold Can Stay" is only eight lines long, a few sentences. It is an apt example of the economic use of words. Each word, each sound, is important.

Yet in that short space, Frost conveys a theme that is a staple of many works of literature: the inevitability of change. *Nothing gold can stay*, he tells us. And this is a theme students can relate to. They see change all around them, in their familes, in their friends. They study it in science, social studies, and literature.

"Nothing Gold Can Stay" is also a good example of how a poet uses the *sound* of language to tell a truth. Frost's use of rhyme, alliteration, and assonance (see page 183) is marvelous and helps hold the poem together.

Companion Poems

Other poems in this book dealing with change or impermanence that can be used in conjunction with "Nothing Gold Can Stay"are:

- "Spring Storm," by Jim Wayne Miller
- "Junkyards," by Julian Lee Rayford
- "Abandoned Farmhouse," by Ted Kooser
- "Deserted Farm," by Mark Vinz

Special Words to Work Through

As he does in many of his poems, Frost keeps his language simple. However, there are a few words and references in "Nothing Good Can Stay" that might need explanation. Students will need know the meaning of *hue* and *subsides*. In addition, they'll need to understand the Biblical story of the Garden of Eden, particularly the part where Adam and Eve are expelled. Even the peace and plenty of paradise didn't last.

THEMES, ISSUES, CONCEPTS

- impermanance
- change(s)

LITERARY TERMS

- figurative language
- sound
- alliteration

ORGANIZERS

- Change

181

FIRST READING: MEETING THE POEM

Write the title of the poem on the board and ask the students what they make of it as a title of a poem. What do they think it means? You might draw their attention to the apparent contradiction: doesn't gold stay gold forever? How can it be that gold cannot/does not stay the same?

After students have suggested some possible explanations, break the class into groups of three or four students and give each group a copy of the **Change** organizer. Have them use it to map out some of their thoughts about cycles and change, which is the theme of Frost's poem.

When the groups have completed their organizers, ask them to give examples of things people do to avoid change. For example, to stay healthy, some people exercise, others take vitamins and supplements. Others choose to have cosmetic surgery in order to remain young looking. Do these practices stop change? Slow it down? Can they think of things that groups—families, teams, nations—do to avoid change?

CLOSE READING: GETTING TO KNOW THE POEM

Theme is one of the more elusive literary terms to define. Consequently, many young readers have difficulty understanding it and knowing its role in a poem. Some students have been taught that theme is the "meaning" of a poem, "what the poet is trying to say." The problem is that explanations like these often distract readers from the *words* of the poem, send them on a detour from experiencing the poem. I've always believed that poetry readers should focus on what the poet *is* saying rather than on what we *think* he or she is "trying to say."

How then to define theme? Most reference works call it the abstract idea made concrete in a poem or work of prose fiction. I like to think of it as a larger truth that an author conveys in a particular work. Looking at the metaphors in "Nothing Gold Can Stay," we see the larger truth that Frost is stating, which is the certainty of impermanence.

An important thing to remember about theme in a work of literature is that it is how *one person* sees the world or a portion of the world. No theme should be taken as a moral certitude. You students should fee free to disagree with how a poet sees the world.

Noticing Figurative Language

We can understand the theme of this short poem by examining its metaphors, especially in the first stanza, where Frost lays out one of his beliefs about life. The metaphors in this poem may be challenging for your more literal-minded students, but you can help them by looking at the stanza line by line and asking some leading questions:

- *Nature's first green is gold.* How can green be gold? It helps if your students understand that gold is a symbol of something precious and valuable. Those first shoots and leaves symbolize rebirth and new life and are equally precious, and therefore *gold.*

- *Her hardest hue to hold.* Frost is not speaking literally, of course. He means that the *first green* is the stage of growth that goes by the most quickly.

- *Her early leaf's a flower;/But only so an hour.* These two lines reinforce what Frost has stated in the title and the opening lines: the quick passing of time, the impermanence of the fresh green shoots and leaves of spring. Again *only an hour* isn't literal; Frost is using hyperbole to make his point.

The first stanza introduces the theme of this poem: things of life change very quickly. Frost continues in this vein in the second stanza with references to Eden ending sadly—it *sank to grief*—and every day passing quickly—*So dawn goes down to day*—and finally his repetition of the title in the final line—*Nothing gold can stay.*

Noticing Sound

Frost does a number of interesting things with sound in this poem. Your students are likely to recognize that the poem is written in couplets—pairs of lines with end rhymes—with the rhyme scheme *aabb ccdd.* These end rhymes help hold the poem together. You should also point out that the final couplet brings the poem to a firm conclusion.

Have your students find the alliteration (repetition of initial consonant sounds) that Frost uses:

- Line 1: *green/gold*
- Line 2: *her/hardest/hue/hold,* continued to line 3: *her*
- Line 7: *dawn, down, day*

He also repeats other sounds skillfully:

- Line 3: *er* in *her early*
- Line 4: *o* in *only so*
- Line 7: *o* in *so/goes*

A master like Frost uses sound to give heft to a poem; we mustn't overlook this as we focus our attention on the meaning of the words.

AFTER READING: KNOWING THE POEM FOREVER

Say It Out Loud

Too many visuals can distract an audience from the performance of a poem, especially a quiet poem like "Nothing Gold Can Stay." However, I think a subdued slide show can be an effective backdrop, especially given the theme of impermanence. A handful of photos that show the change of seasons, for example, would do nicely.

As far as performing the poem, I see the even-numbered lines as responses to the odd-numbered lines; it can therefore be performed by two voices:

Nature's first green is gold,

> Her hardest hue to hold,

Her early leaf's a flower;

> But only so an hour.

Then leaf subsides to leaf.

> So Eden sank to grief,

So dawn goes down to day.

> Nothing gold can stay.

It can also be performed by two small choruses, say eight students in each, each group reciting one line.

Write About It

Have students explore one of these ideas in their writer's notebook:

1. Write about something you thought would never change but did, in fact, change. Was it a change for the better? Or did it make you feel sad, angry, betrayed?

2. If you live in a part of the country that experiences a change of seasons, write a short personal narrative that shows the change you like the most or the least and why.

3. If you live in a place that does not experience significant seasonal changes, write about your reasons for liking/disliking that. If you wish you could experience a significant change of seasons, write about why.

4. Make a list of things you wish would never change.

Issues/Themes/Topics for Discussion

- Change
- Impermanence
- Trying to hold on to something/someone
- Changing friendships

Related Poems

"I Still Have Everything You Gave Me," by Naomi Shihab Nye

"Enchantment," by Joanne Ryder

"The Poem That Got Away," by Felice Holman

"The Changeling," by Siv Cedering

"The Christmas Cactus," by Liz Rosenberg

Book Bridges

I Found a Dead Bird: The Kids' Guide to the Cycle of Life and Death by Jan Thornhill. A book that explores the cycle of life and death in nature, while exploring how death affects all of us and offering some strategies for coping with a death.

Each Little Bird that Sings by Deborah Wiles. Comfort Snowberger's family runs a funeral home in their small southern town. Even though Comfort has been around death, she is unprepared for the sudden death of her beloved uncle.

Online Resources

- You will have no trouble finding information about Robert Frost, who is an American icon. A great place to start is at the Frost page on the website of the Academy of American Poets (www.poets.org/poet.php/prmPID/192). Not only does the page contain biographical information about Frost, there is also a good introductory selection of his poems. One of the external links is to "A Frost Bouquet," which includes many illustrations and photographs related to the poet and his family.

- Another worthwhile link is www.frostfriends.org, which includes a chronology, a reading list, a biography, and The Robert Frost Tutorial "for students with questions."

Name _____ Date _____ Class _____

Change _____

Make a list of things that change—big things or little things. The change can be a quick change—your friend suddenly isn't your friend—or a gradual change—a change of season.

Once you have a list of between fifteen and twenty things that change, organize them into categories. For instance, you might have a group of items that relate to the physical body or sports. Use a different box for each category.

A Few Final Words

My hopes for this book are many. I hope that, like your classes, this book will be a work-in-progress for you. I hope you have found much in here that is helpful to you in making poetry a lively and continuing presence in your classes. I hope that your writer's notebook has grown fat with new poems, new ideas, and new enthusiasm. More than anything else, however, I hope you and your students come to embrace the words of Philip Booth, who said that a good poem "makes the world more habitable." Any good poem, he went on to say, "changes the world. It changes the world slightly in favor of being alive and being human."